INSTRUCTOR'S
RESOURCE
MANUAL

HUMAN
RESOURCE
MANAGEMENT

**INSTRUCTOR'S MANUAL,
EXERCISE NOTES, AND
<u>SKILLS LIVE! VIDEO NOTES</u>**

Jay Hochstetler
Ivy Tech State College

**EXPERIENTIAL EXERCISES,
CASE NOTES, AND SB2000
<u>VIDEO NOTES</u>**

George M. Puia
Indiana State University

<u>With contributions by</u>

John E. Oliver
Valdosta State University

Elisa Adams

HUMAN RESOURCE MANAGEMENT

EIGHTH EDITION

GARY DESSLER

PRENTICE HALL
UPPER SADDLE RIVER, NJ 07458

Acquisitions editor: Stephanie Johnson
Managing editor: Melissa Steffens
Associate editor: Hersch Doby
Project editor: Richard Bretan
Manufacturer: Victor Graphics, Inc.

Printed in the United States of America

10 9 8 7 6 5 4 3 2 1

ISBN 0-13-016355-4

Prentice-Hall International (UK) Limited, London
Prentice-Hall of Australia Pty. Limited, Sydney
Prentice-Hall Canada Inc., Toronto
Prentice-Hall Hispanoamericana, S.A., Mexico
Prentice-Hall of India Private Limited, New Delhi
Prentice-Hall of Japan, Inc., Tokyo
Prentice-Hall (Singapore) Pte Ltd
Editora Prentice-Hall do Brasil, Ltda., Rio de Janeiro

TABLE OF CONTENTS

Introduction

This instructor's manual is designed for use with Gary Dessler's *Human Resource Management,* 8th edition. I believe that the most valuable learning comes through interaction with a well-prepared, enthusiastic and knowledgeable instructor. In preparing this instructor's manual, I have attempted to make it flexible and useful for a wide variety of experience levels.

Organization of this Manual

Each chapter section begins with *In Brief* and *Interesting Issues* sections that give a summary of what the chapter is about and the issues related to today's business world. A *Lecture Outline* represents the bulk of each chapter section. References are made to figures in the text to allow you to integrate them in your lecture. The lecture outline is followed by a description of the *Discussion Boxes* that are contained in the chapter.

Each chapter of the text has a list of *Key Terms*. This manual pulls the definition of each term from the chapter for you and provides you with the page on which that definition is found. This is followed with answers to the *Discussion Questions* from the text. When appropriate, page references for the applicable text section are given. Some questions are designed to encourage discussion and have no single "correct" answer.

Included at the end of the text chapters are *Experiential Exercises*, *Case Incidents* and *Case Applications*. Each **exercise** or **case** is reviewed and suggestions are given for your in-class discussion of case-related questions. Consider using at least one of the application exercises with each chapter as they give the students a chance to apply the concepts. As with some of the discussion questions, cases generally do not have "correct" answers, but can generate meaningful discussion that helps the student to grasp the concepts.

A number of videos have been selected and provided for your use in the classroom. The **Video Guide** gives you a brief summary of the two sets of videos to accompany this text – the custom-created and skill-oriented *Skills Live!,* and the company cases from *Small Business 2000.* The Video Guide provides short descriptions of each video segment, gives the run-time, and provides handouts with questions based on the video for the students to answer. For the *Skills Live!* video, it is suggested that you let the students try to answer the questions in groups. Stop the *Skills Live!* video following each skit-ending questioning phase for students to answer. Then re-start the video. Author Gary Dessler will then provide students with the suggested answers.

Special thanks go to George M. Puia of Indiana State University for his contributions to the cases and exercises in both the text and this Instructor's Manual. George also provided editing instructions for the PBS *SB2000* tapes and wrote the video case notes and discussion questions for the *SB2000* portion of the Video Guide. Special thanks also go to Elisa Adams and John E. Oliver of Valdosta State University for his permission to use some of his case examples.

Teaching and the Experienced Student

The demographic make-up of the college classroom is changing. Many students are entering the classroom with some significant work experience. As an instructor, it is important to recognize and use the knowledge and diverse experiences present in your classroom. If you have students with significant work experience, it may be very useful to initiate classroom discussions that will allow them to share how they have witnessed human resource management issues and practices in action. Their experiences will illustrate how the chapter concepts were or were not practiced sufficiently in their organizations.

Using the Internet with this Book

I strongly encourage you to utilize the *HRM*, 8/e website at **http://www.prenhall.com/dessler**. Professor Dan Cooper of Marist College and his folks at PHLIP, Prentice Hall Learning on the Internet Partnership, have combined content and multimedia on this website to provide you and your students with exceptional academic support. This site has Internet exercises for each chapter and there are monthly updates based on current events. This is an excellent tool to keep your teaching current and to give assignments involving Internet sources to keep your students interested and excited.

Thanks also go to Mary Gowan of the University of Central Florida for her work on the student Study Guide and its web companion, and Thomas Patterson for his PowerPoint electronic transparencies. Both supplements can be accessed through the website.

Jay Hochstetler
Marion, IN

Chapter 1
The Strategic Role of Human Resource Management

In Brief: This chapter gives an overview of what HR is, its changing environment, and the role of HR in strategic planning.

Interesting Issues: A major issue is the changing role of HR in organizations. Where HR was once a clerical function that was relegated to the lower echelons of the organization, today more and more companies have elevated the HR function to an integral part of the senior planning team. Having students research and show these types of changes in organizations may be a useful and important learning tool.

Lecture Outline

I. **Human Resource Management at Work**

    A.   What is Human Resource Management?

        1.   There are five basic functions of management: planning, organizing, staffing, leading, and controlling.

        2.   HR is the staffing function of management.

        3.   HRM refers to the practices and policies you need to carry out the people or personnel aspects of your management job. These include:

               a.   conducting job analysis
               b.   planning labor needs
               c.   selecting job candidates
               d.   orienting and training new employees
               e.   managing wages and salaries
               f.   providing incentives and benefits
               g.   appraising performance
               h.   communicating
               i.   training and developing
               j.   building employee commitment

        4.   What a manager should know about:

               a.   equal opportunity and affirmative action
               b.   employee health and safety
               c.   grievances and labor relations

    B.   Why is HR Management Important to All Managers?

Chapter 1: The Strategic Role of Human Resource Management

      1.   Helps you avoid common personnel mistakes:

            a.   hiring the wrong person for the job
            b.   experiencing high turnover
            c.   finding your people not doing their best
            d.   wasting time with useless interviews
            e.   having your company taken to court because of your discriminatory actions
            f.   having your company cited under federal occupational safety laws for unsafe practices
            g.   having some of your employees think their salaries are unfair and inequitable relative to others in the organization
            h.   allowing a lack of training to undermine your department's effectiveness.
            i.   committing any unfair labor practices

      2.   Helps you ensure you get results - through others.

C.   Line and Staff Aspects of HRM

D.   Line Versus Staff Authority

      1.   Authority is the right to make decisions, to direct the work of others and to give orders.

      2.   Line managers are authorized to direct the work of subordinates.

      3.   Staff managers are authorized to assist and advise line managers.

E.   Line Managers' Human Resource Management Responsibilities

      1.   Placement

      2.   Orientation

      3.   Training

      4.   Improving job performance

      5.   gaining creative cooperation

      6.   interpreting policies and procedures

      7.   controlling labor costs

      8.   developing employee abilities

      9.   creating and maintaining departmental morale

          10.   protecting employees' health and physical condition

    F.   Human Resource Department's HR Management Responsibilities

          1.   The HR manager carries out three distinct functions:

               a.   line function
               b.   coordinative function
               c.   staff (service) functions

          2.   Figure 1-1 on page 6 of the text has a sample organizational chart which serves as a summary of the HR positions you might find in a large company. It might be worthwhile to make sure that students understand that not all companies will be organized in this way. Some may have other functions under the HR area, and sometimes the functions listed may not be under the HR area.

    G.   Cooperative Line and Staff Human Resource Management: An Example

        Figure 1-2 on page 7 of the text gives an example of how a company might divide activities between line managers and the HR department. Again, it should be pointed out that different companies might divide these activities differently.

        Table 1-1 on pages 8 & 9 of the text shows how the HR activities are divided between the HR department and other departments based on a recent survey. This will be helpful for student to realize that most functions are shared between the HR and other departments.

II.   The Changing Environment of Human Resource Management

    A.   Globalization

          1.   tendency of firms to extend their sales or manufacturing to new markets

          2.   manufacturers putting facilities where they will be most advantageous

    B.   Technological Trends

          1. Communications

          2. Telecommuting

          3. CAD/CAM and Robotics

          4. Impact on jobs and organizational charts

  C. Deregulation

  D. Trends in the Nature of Work

    1. Shift from manufacturing to service jobs.

    2. Rising premium on human capital.

    3. New methods needed to win employee commitment.

  E. Workforce Diversity

    1. Diversity is "...any attribute that humans are likely to use to tell themselves, 'that person is different from me.'" and includes:

      a. race
      b. sex
      c. age
      d. values
      e. cultural norms
      f. etc.

    2. The make-up of the work force is rapidly changing.

      a. more women, including single mothers
      b. dramatic changes in racial composition
      c. age: more older workers

    3. The increases in work force diversity will provide many challenges for HR management.

      a. increased health care costs
      b. more benefits such as free time are demanded
      c. child care issues
      d. travel, scheduling, & moving needs of dual-career families
      e. creating a cohesive and collegial work force

  E. Legal Trends Affecting Human Resource Management

III. **Tomorrow's HR Today**

  A. New Management Practices

    1. Rapid change creates a need for responsive organizations.

    2. The traditional, pyramid-shaped organization is going out of style.

    3. Employees are being empowered.

        4.   Flatter organizations are becoming the norm.

        5.   Work is increasingly organized around teams and processes.

        6.   The bases of power are changing.

        7.   Managers today must build commitment.

Figure 1-3 on page 14 describes some of the fundamental changes facing managers today.

Case Study: The High Performing Organization: Building Better, Faster, More Competitive Organizations Through HR. This case study on pages 15 & 16 outlines how Asea Brown Boveri put these kinds of changes into practice.

    B.   The Changing Role of HR Management

        1.   History of Personnel / HR

             a.   began in early 1900s - primarily procedural
             b.   increasing role due to technology such as testing
             c.   union legislation in the 1930s
             d.   discrimination legislation in the 1960s and 1970s
             e.   shifting from protector & screener to planner & change agent

Figure 1-4 on page 17 show the results of a survey on what CEOs said they are spending their time doing. Reshaping corporate culture and employee behavior rated in the top 3.

        2.   HR and Employee Commitment

        3.   HR and Performance

             a.   HR and service
             b.   HR and responsiveness
             c.   HR research insight

        4.   HR and Corporate Strategy

IV.   Strategic Planning and HR Management

    A.   The Nature of Strategic Planning

        1.   Three levels of strategic planning:

             a.   corporate strategy
             b.   business-level/competitive strategy
             c.   functional strategies

Chapter 1: The Strategic Role of Human Resource Management

      2.   Building competitive advantage

          a.   cost leadership
          b.   differentiation

      3.   Human Resources as a Competitive Advantage

Figure 1-5 on page 20 describes the relationships among strategies in multiple-business firms.

  B.   Strategic Human Resource Management

      1.   "...the linking of HRM with strategic goals and objectives in order to improve business performance and develop organizational cultures that foster innovation and flexibility ..."

      2.   HR Strategies refers to the specific HR courses of action the company plans to pursue to achieve its aims.

Figure 1-6 on page 22 illustrates the interplay between HR strategy and the company's business plans and results.

  C.   HR's Role as a Strategic Partner

      1.   Three views of HR.

          a.   strictly operational and not strategic
          b.   role is to "fit" the company's strategy
          c.   equal partner in the strategic planning process

      2.   HR's role in formulating strategy

          a.   environmental scanning
          b.   competitive intelligence
          c.   internal strengths & weaknesses analysis
          d.   development of an HR-based competitive advantage

      3.   HR's role in executing strategy

      4.   HR. practices: Is there a "one best way?"

      5.   The strategic future of the HR department

Key Terms

management process	The five basic functions of management are: planning, organizing, staffing, leading, and controlling. (page 2)
human resource management	The staffing function of the management process. Or, the policies and practices needed to carry out the "people" or human resource aspects of a management position, including recruiting, screening, training, rewarding, and appraising. (page 2)
authority	The right to make decisions, to direct the work of others, and to give orders. (page 3)
line manager	Authorized to direct the work of subordinates-they're always someone's boss. In addition, line managers are in charge of accomplishing the organization's basic goals. (page 3)
staff manager	Assist and advise line managers in accomplishing the basic goals. HR managers are generally staff managers. (page 4)
line authority	The authority to direct the activities of the people in his or her own department. (page 4)
implied authority	The authority exerted by virtue of others' knowledge that he or she has access to top management. (page 4)
functional control	The authority exerted by a personnel manager as a coordinator of personnel activities. (page 4)
employee advocacy	HR must take responsibility for clearly defining how management should be treating employees, make sure employees have the mechanisms required to contest unfair practices, and represent the interests of employees within the framework of its primary obligation to senior management. (page 5)
globalization	The tendency of firms to extend their sales or manufacturing to new markets abroad. (page 9)
competitive advantage	Factors that allow an organization to differentiate its product or service from competitors to increase market share. (page 21)
cost leadership	The enterprise aims to become the low-cost leader in an industry. (page 21)
differentiation	A firm seeks to be unique in its industry along dimensions that are widely valued by buyers. (page 21)

Discussion Questions:

1. Explain what HR management is and how it relates to the management process.
There are five basic functions that all managers perform: planning, organizing, staffing, leading, and controlling. HR management involves the policies and practices needed to carry out the staffing (or people) function of management. HR management helps the management process avoid mistakes and to get results. (pages 2-3)

2. Give several examples of how HR management concepts and techniques can be of use to all managers. HR management concepts and techniques can help all managers to ensure that they get results--through others. These concepts and techniques also help avoid common personnel mistakes listed at the bottom of page 2 and the top of page 3 in the text. Students should list several of these as examples. (pages 2-3)

3. Compare and contrast the work of line and staff managers; give examples of each.
Line managers are someone's boss; they direct the work of subordinates in pursuit of accomplishing the organization's basic goals. Staff managers assist and advise line managers in accomplishing these basic goals. They do, however, need to work in partnership with each other to be successful. (pages 3-8)

4. Why is it important for a company to make its human resources into a competitive advantage? How can HR contribute to doing so? Building and maintaining a competitive advantage is what allows a company to be successful, and to remain profitable and in business. HR can make a critical contribution to the competitive advantage of a company by building the organizational climate and structure that allows the company to tap its special skills or core competencies and rapidly respond to customers' needs and competitors' moves. (page 21)

5. What is meant by strategic human resource management and what exactly is HR's role in the strategic planning process? "...the linking of HRM with strategic goals and objectives in order to improve business performance and develop organizational cultures that foster innovation and flexibility ..."
The role of HR in the strategic planning process depends on the organization's view of HR. There are three views detailed on page 23 of the text which involve HR as an operational function, HR as a "fitting" function, and HR as an equal partner in the strategic planning process. Obviously, it is our contention that the latter is the appropriate view. In this view, HR's role would include environmental scanning, competitive intelligence, internal strengths and weaknesses analysis, and the implementation of the strategies. (pages 21-26)

Individual and Group Activities:

1. **Working individually or in groups, develop several lists showing how trends like work force diversity, technological trends, globalization, and changes in the nature of work have affected the college or university you are now attending.** The list might include items such as the growth of adult (non-traditional aged) students, the use of computer and communications technology, diversity issues, and others.

2. **Working individually or in groups, develop a list of examples showing how the new management practices discussed in this chapter (worker empowerment, flatter organizations, and so on) have or have not been implemented to some extent in the college or university you are now attending, or in the organization for which you work.** The lists should be specific examples of changes that have occurred in the organization as evidence of the management practices mentioned.

3. **Working individually or in groups, interview an HR manager; based on that interview write a short presentation regarding HR's role today in building a more responsive organization.** The response here will, of course, depend upon the organization and HR manager interviewed. Hopefully items such as work force diversity, technological trends, globalization, organizational structures, empowerment, teams, or employee commitment will be mentioned.

Cases and Exercises

Experiential Exercise: HRM As A Strategic Partner in Strategic Planning (page 29)

Examples of possible answers to the critical issues are:

Critical Issue	Effect on existing employees	Potential HR role(s)
(Example) 1. Distance learning technology	*(Example)* Need for better computer skills.	*(Example)* Provide greater technical training.
2. Government reductions in funding to higher education	Less money for raises – potential turnover	Focus on HR programs that increase job satisfaction. Improvements in productivity.
3. Greater workforce diversity	Current employees may have communication difficulties; culture shock	Diversity training needs will increase
4. More international students	Greater classroom diversity; communication challenge.	Cross cultural training for faculty. Orientation for International students.
5. High percentage of faculty to retire over next decade.	More faculty will be needed	Recruiting program to attract faculty. Retention program for existing faculty. Retirement programs for retirees.

6. Local large business is developing its own corporate university.	May draw faculty to the corporate university.	Employee retention programs.

Questions:

1. Which environmental change would have the greatest impact on the human resource needs of the university? Students will form their own opinions (there is no right answer). Probe students as to how they reached their decision. Most likely either the reductions in government funding or the local business will develop its own corporate university.

2. What environmental change will be the most difficult for your HR group to manage? You should expect a range of responses based on local conditions. Diversity will likely surface as a major issue. Any of the critical issues could top this chart. Look for good rationale that displays an understanding of the complications that each one presents for a HR staff.

3. Overall, how will this combination of changes affect your organization? Bright students will consider issues like the staffing level of the current HR organization. Some may raise the issue of "who trains the trainers?" Students should note that in every environmental change, there are some effect on the HR needs of the organization and therefore on the HR department itself. These changes will force the organization to become more responsive and proactive to change, and focused on meeting the competitive challenges of the environment.

Case Incident: Jack Nelson's Problem (page 30)

1. What do you think was causing some of the problems in the savings and loan home office and branches? There is clearly a problem with communication, and the effects are felt in the area of employee commitment. Additional contributing factors include the lack of consistency in the policies and procedures of various locations. There is no cohesiveness to the staffing activities of this organization.

2. Do you think setting up a HR unit in the main office would help? Of course we think it would! Since there are HR-related problems both in the home office and in the branches, it is clear that if a personnel office were set up, it would need to help to coordinate the HR activities in the branches.

3. What specific functions should it carry out? What HR functions would then be carried out by supervisors and other line managers? There is room for quite a bit of variation in the answers to this question. Our suggested organization would include:

HR Unit: job analyses, planning labor needs and recruiting, providing advising and training in the selection process, orientation of new employees, managing wage and salary administration, managing incentives and benefits, providing and managing the performance appraisal process, organization-wide communications, and providing training & developing services.

Supervisors and Other Line Managers: interviewing and selection of job candidates, training new employees, appraising performance, departmental & personal communications, and training & development.

Case Application: Turnover in the Bank (page 30)

The Conservative State Savings Bank was a medium sized bank located in a large southern city. A sizeable unit of the bank, the check processing department, was staffed by women aged eighteen to forty. The department had been experiencing an annual turnover rate of about 40 percent, greatly reducing operating efficiency.

1. **What were some of the possible problem Juanita Nelson found in her investigation of employee turnover?** The employees provided a variety of reasons (many of which were different or more detailed then they provided at the time of their departure). Among the problems employees mentioned were: boring work, impersonal treatment, inflexible work schedules (including weekend work), compensation issues (amount and confidentiality), supervisor indifference, "forced contribution" to the company's charitable fund, and poor supervision. One employee even suggested the company needed a union.

2. **Should Nelson also survey the supervisors before making recommendations?** Absolutely! First, Nelson has only heard one side of the story. While there is great consistency between employee accounts, the stories also lack a management perspective. Second, any solution that Nelson recommends will need the support of management. She needs to understand what has stood in the way of supervisors being more effective in their jobs.

3. **Based on the case, what role(s) could the HR department beyond recruiting?** A number of strategic roles for HR are implicitly identified in the case including: quality of worklife measurement, job design, employee selection (matching employees skills to jobs), training employees, supervisory training, compensation plans, and labor relations. HR could be a significant advisor to operations – improving the quality and efficiency of the work while also becoming a better workplace for employees.

Chapter 2
Equal Opportunity and the Law

In Brief: This chapter gives a history of equal opportunity legislation, outlines defenses against discrimination allegations, gives examples of discriminatory practices, describes the EEOC enforcement process and suggests proactive programs.

Interesting Issues: Affirmative Action programs have come under fire in recent years, even by some members of protected groups. A very critical issue is whether Affirmative Action represents a "leg up" assistance for those who have been historically discriminated against, or if it becomes a "crutch" that hinders their motivation and ability to compete and perform. While this is a delicate and potentially volatile issue, helping students be able to see and understand both sides of the argument will help them understand the depth of these issues.

Lecture Outline

I. **Equal Employment Opportunity 1964-1991**

    A.   Background

    B.   Title VII of the 1964 Civil Rights Act

        1.   Says it is unlawful:

            a.   to fail or refuse to hire or to discharge an individual or otherwise to discriminate against any individual with respect to his/her compensation, terms, conditions, or privileges of employment, because of such individual's race, color, religion, sex, or national origin.

            b.   to limit, segregate, or classify his/her employees or applicants for employment in any way that would deprive or tend to deprive any individual of employment opportunities or otherwise adversely affect his/her status as an employee, because of such individual's race, color, religion, sex, or national origin.

        2.   Who does Title VII Cover?

            a.   all public or private employers of 15 or more persons

            b.   all private and public educational institutions

            c.   the federal, state, and local governments

            d.   public and private employment agencies

            e.   labor unions with 15 or more members

            f.   joint labor-management committees

         3.   The EEOC

                a.   investigates job discrimination complaints
                b.   may file charges in court

C.   Executive Orders

D.   Equal Pay Act of 1963

E.   Age Discrimination in Employment Act of 1967

F.   Vocational Rehabilitation Act of 1973

         1.   Required Employers with Federal Contracts over $2500 to take Affirmative Action for Handicapped People.

         2.   Was Used to Help Outlaw Discrimination Against People with AIDS.

G.   Vietnam Era Veterans' Readjustment Assistance Act of 1974

H.   Pregnancy Discrimination Act of 1978

I.   Federal Agency Guidelines

         1.   Uniform Guidelines on Employee Selection Procedures

         2.   EEOC Guidelines

J.   Sexual Harassment

         1.   Unwelcome sexual advances, requests for favors and other verbal or physical conduct of a sexual nature that takes place under any of the following conditions:

                a.   submission to such conduct is made either explicitly or implicitly a term or condition of an individual's employment
                b.   submission to or rejection of such conduct by an individual is used as the basis for employment decisions affecting such individual
                c.   such conduct has the purpose or effect of unreasonably interfering with an individual's work performance or creating an intimidating, hostile, or offensive work environment

         2.   Quid Pro Quo

         3.   Hostile Environment Created by Supervisors

         4.   Hostile Environment Created by Coworkers or Non-employees

         5.   What the Employer Should Do: see list on pages 43 & 44

6. What the Employee Can Do: see list of steps on page 44

K. Selected Early Court Decisions Regarding Equal Employment Opportunity

1. *Griggs v. Duke Power Company*

   a. defined unfair discrimination

2. *Albemarle Paper Company v. Moody*

   a. screening tools must be job related or valid

II. **Equal Employment Opportunity 1989-1991: A Shifting Supreme Court**

A. Shift to narrower scope for civil rights protection

B. *Price Waterhouse v. Hopkins*

C. *Wards Cove Packing Company v. Atonio*

III. **Equal Employment Opportunity 1991-Present**

A. The Civil Rights Act of 1991

1. Burden of Proof (Wards Cove)

2. Money Damages

3. Mixed Motives (Price Waterhouse)

4. Proof of Discrimination

5. Global HRM: Enforcing the 1991 Civil Rights Act Abroad page 48 of text; see Discussion Boxes solutions

B. The American with Disabilities Act

1. Legal Obligations of Employers: see pages 49- 50 of text

2. ADA in Practice

C. State and Local Equal Employment Opportunity Laws

D. Summary

Table 2.1 on page 52 of the text gives a good summary outline of the names of the various actions and what they do.

IV.   Defenses Against Discrimination Allegations

    A.   What is Adverse Impact?

    B.   How can Adverse Impact be Proved?

        1.   Disparate Rejection Rates

        2.   Restricted Policy

        3.   Population Comparisons

        4.   *McDonnell-Douglas* Test

        5.   Bringing a Case of Discrimination: Summary

    B.   Bona Fide Occupational Qualification (BFOQ)

        1.   Age as a BFOQ

            a.   Narrowing of exceptions
            b.   FOA: factors other than age

        2.   Religion as a BFOQ

        3.   Gender as a BFOQ

        4.   National Origin as a BFOQ

    C.   Business Necessity

    D.   Other Considerations in Discriminatory Practice Defenses

V.   Illustrative Discriminatory Employment Practices

    A.   A Note on What You Cannot Do

    B.   Recruitment

        1.   Word of Mouth

        2.   Misleading Information

        3.   Help Wanted Ads

    C.   Selection Standards

Chapter 2: Equal Opportunity and the Law

        1.   Educational Requirements

        2.   Tests

        3.   Preference to Relatives

        4.   Height, Weight, and Physical Characteristics

        5.   Arrest Records

        6.   Discharge Due to Garnishment

D.   Sample Discriminatory Promotion, Transfer, and Layoff Practices

        1.   Personal Appearance Regulations and Title VII

        2.   Dress

        3.   Grooming

        4.   Hair

        5.   Uniforms

VI.   The EEOC Enforcement Process

A.   Processing a Charge

     Figure 2.2 on page 61 gives a good list of questions to ask when an employer receives notice that a bias complaint has been filed

B.   Conciliation Proceedings

C.   How to Respond to Employment Discrimination Charges

        1.   Investigating the Charge

        2.   The Fact-Finding Conference

E.   The EEOC's Determination and the Attempted Conciliation

F.   Avoiding Discrimination Lawsuits Through Dispute Resolution

G.   Mandatory Arbitration of Employment Discrimination Claims

H.   The High-Performance Organization: A Paperless EEO Complaint Process. page 65 of text; see Discussion Boxes solutions

VII. Diversity Management and Affirmative Action Programs

    A.   Managing Diversity

    B.   Boosting Workforce Diversity

    B.   Equal Employment Opportunity Versus Affirmative Action

    C.   Steps in an Affirmative Action Program

        1.   The Eight Steps (pages 68 & 69)

        2.   Sample Affirmative Action Report (figure 2.4 on page 69)

    D.   Affirmative Action: Two Basic Strategies

        1.   Good Faith Effort Strategy

        2.   Quota Strategy

            a.   *Wygant v. Jackson Board of Education*
            b.   *Local 28 Sheet Metal Workers v. EEOC*
            c.   *International Association of Firefighters v. The City of Cleveland*
            d   *U.S. v. Paradise*
            e.   *Johnson v. Transportation Agency, Santa Clara County*

        3.   A Practical Approach

Discussion Boxes

Global HRM: Enforcing the 1991 Civil Rights Act Abroad
(page 48)

This discussion box highlights the effort of this law to include coverage of "U.S. citizens employed in a foreign country by a U.S.-owned or U.S.-controlled company." The law's bark will be worse than its bite because: 1) There are numerous exceptions, including when compliance would cause the employer to violate the host country's law, 2) Investigators are not trained for some of the types of investigations they are expected to do, and 3) Few foreign countries will cooperate with the intrusive enforcement of U.S. civil law in their jurisdiction.

The High Performance Organization: Building Better, Faster, More Competitive Organizations Through: A Paperless EEO Complaint Process
(page 65)

     This describes Rock Island Arsenal's (RIA) implementation of a new computer system designed to automate the processing of EEO complaints. The system eliminates misfiling and misplaced documents. It provides increased accessibility, greater security, and reduced overall processing costs.

Key Terms

Title VII of the 1964 Civil Rights Act	The section of the act that says an employer cannot discriminate on the basis of race, religion, sex, or national origin with respect to employment. (page 37)
EEOC	The commission, created by Title VII, is empowered to investigate job discrimination complaints and sue on behalf of complainants. (page 38)
affirmative action	Steps that are taken for the purpose of eliminating the present effects of past discrimination. (page 38)
OFCCP	This office is responsible for implementing the executive orders and ensuring compliance of federal contractors. (page 38)
Equal Pay Act of 1963	The act requiring equal pay for equal work, regardless of sex. (page 38)
Age Discrimination in Employment Act of 1967	The act prohibiting arbitrary age discrimination and specifically protecting individuals over 40 years old. (page 38)
Voc. Rehab. Act of 1973	The act requiring certain federal contractors to take affirmative action for disabled persons. (page 39)
Vietnam Era Veterans' Readjustment Act - 1974	The act that requires employers with government contracts of $10,000 or more to take affirmative action to employ and advance disabled veterans and qualified veterans of the Vietnam era. The act is administered by the OFCCP. (page 39)
Pregnancy Discrimination Act (PDA)	An amendment to Title VII of the Civil Rights Act that prohibits sex discrimination based on "pregnancy, childbirth, or related medical conditions." (page 39)

federal agency guidelines	Guidelines issued by federal agencies charged with ensuring compliance with federal equal employment legislation explaining recommended employer procedures in detail. (page 40)
sexual harassment	Harassment on the basis of sex that has the purpose or effect of substantially interfering with a person's work performance or creating an intimidating, hostile, or offensive work environment. (page 40)
Meritor Savings Bank v. Vinson	U.S. Supreme Court's first decision on sexual harassment holding that existence of a hostile environment even without economic hardship is sufficient to prove harassment, even if participation was voluntary. (page 42)
Griggs v. Duke Power	Case heard by the Supreme Court in which the plaintiff argued that his employer's requirement that coal handlers be high school graduates was unfairly discriminatory. In finding for the plaintiff, the Court ruled that discrimination need not be overt to be illegal, that employment practices must be related to job performance, and that the burden of proof is on the employer to show that hiring standards are job related. (page 45)
protected class	Persons such as minorities and women protected by equal opportunity laws including Title VII. (page 45)
Albemarle Paper Co. v. Moody	Supreme Court case in which it was ruled that the validity of job tests must be documented and that employee performance standards must be unambiguous. (page 45)
Wards Cove v. Atonio	U.S. Supreme Court decision that makes it more difficult to prove a case of unlawful discrimination against an employer. Under this ruling, statistical imbalances themselves do not demonstrate disparate impact; instead the employee/applicant must prove that the statistical imbalances were caused by an employment policy or practice of the employer. (pages 46)
Civil Rights Act of 1991	This act places the burden of proof back on employers and permits compensatory and punitive damages. (pages 47)
Americans with Disabilities Act	The act requiring employers to make reasonable accommodation for disabled employees. It prohibits discrimination against disabled persons. (page 48)
adverse impact	The overall impact of employer practices that result in significantly higher percentages of members of minorities and other protected groups being rejected for employment, placement, or promotion. (pages 51)

disparate rejection rates
One test for adverse impact in which it can be demonstrated that there is a discrepancy between rates of rejection of members of a protected group and of others. (page 53)

restricted policy
Another test for adverse impact, involving demonstration that an employer's hiring practices exclude a protected group, whether intentionally or not. (page 53)

BFOQ
Bona Fide Occupational Qualification. Requirement that an employee be of a certain religion, sex, or national origin where that is reasonably necessary to the organization's normal operation. Specified by the 1964 Civil Rights Act. (pages 54)

business necessity
Justification for an otherwise discriminatory employment practice, provided there is an overriding legitimate business purpose. (page 56)

good faith effort strategy
One of two basic affirmative action plan strategies. This emphasizes identifying and eliminating the obstacles to hiring and promoting women and minorities on the assumption that eliminating these obstacles will result in increased utilization of women and minorities. (page 69)

quota strategy
One of two basic affirmative action plan strategies. This strategy mandates bottom line results by instituting hiring and promotion restrictions. (page 69)

reverse discrimination
Claim that, due to affirmative action quota systems, white males are discriminated against. (page 70)

Discussion Questions:

1. **What are the main EEO laws and what do they say?**
An excellent summary of the EEO laws and what they say is Table 2-1 on page 52.

2. **What important precedents were set by the *Griggs v. Duke Power Company* case?**
Case heard by the Supreme Court in which the plaintiff argued that his employer's requirement that coal handlers be high school graduates was unfairly discriminatory. In finding for the plaintiff, the Court ruled that discrimination need not be overt to be illegal, that employment practices must be related to job performance, and that the burden of proof is on the employer to show that hiring standards are job related. (page 45)

   The *Albemarle v. Moody* case? Supreme Court case in which it was ruled that the validity of job tests must be documented and that employee performance standards must be unambiguous. (page 45)

3. **What is adverse impact? How can it be proven?** The overall impact of employer practices that result in significantly higher percentages of members of minorities and other protected groups being rejected for employment, placement, or promotion. The complainant need only establish a prima facie case: showing that the employer's selection procedures did have an adverse impact on a protected minority group. This is done by one of four basic approaches: disparate rejection rates; the restricted policy approach; population comparisons; the *McDonnell-Douglas* Test. (pages 51)

Individual and Group Activities:

1. **Assume you are a supervisor on an assembly line: you are responsible for hiring subordinates, supervising them, and recommending them for promotion. Working individually or in groups, compile a list of discriminatory management practices you should avoid.** Word of mouth hiring, misleading information, improper help wanted adds, invalid educational requirements, invalid tests, preferences to relatives, non-job related height, weight, and physical characteristic requirements, use of arrest records, discharge due to garnishment, etc. (pages 57-59)

2. **Working individually or in groups, discuss how you would set up an affirmative action program.** It is important that students reach a decision of whether to use the good faith effort strategy or the quota strategy. Most experts would suggest the good faith effort strategy is the most legally acceptable approach. The list of six actions on page 71 should be demonstrated in the student plans. (pages 69-71)

3. **Compare and contrast the issues presented in *Bakke* and *Weber* with new court rulings on affirmative action. Working individually or in groups, discuss the current direction of affirmative action as a policy in light of the *Johnson* ruling?** The basic questions addressed in *Bakke* and *Weber* focused on when preferential treatment becomes discrimination and under what circumstances discrimination will be temporarily permitted. Neither question was fully answered. Subsequent cases have continued to address these issues and clarify more specifically the scope and intent of affirmative action. For example, in the *Paradise* case, the court ruled that the courts can impose racial quotas to address the most serious cases of racial discrimination. In *Johnson*, the court ruled that the public and private employers may voluntarily adopt hiring and promotion goals to benefit minorities and women. The *Johnson* ruling may limit claims of reverse discrimination by white males. (page 70)

4. **Explain the defenses and exceptions to discriminatory practice allegations.** There are two basic defenses where a prima facie case has been shown: 1) BFOQ - if the employer can show that religion, sex, or national origin is a necessary requirement to do the job, or 2) business necessity - there is an overriding business purpose for the practice. (pages 54-56)

5. **What is the difference between affirmative action and equal employment opportunity?** Equal employment opportunity aims to ensure that anyone, regardless of race, color, sex, religion, national origin, or age has an equal chance for a job based on his or her qualifications. Affirmative action requires the employer to make an extra effort to hire and

promote those in protected groups and includes specific actions designed to eliminate the present effects of past discrimination. (page 38)

6. **Explain how the 1991 Civil Rights Act "turned back the clock" on equal employment Supreme Court cases decided from 1989 to 1991.** Supreme court rulings such as *Wards Cove* and *Patterson* had the effect of limiting the protection of women and minority groups under equal employment laws. The Civil Rights Act of 1991 basically reversed several Supreme Court rulings and added the following: shifted burden of proof to the employer, allowed money damages, applied the Civil Rights Act of 1866 to discrimination after hiring, allowed findings of discrimination even with mixed motives, gave more protection to consent decrees, and extended coverage to U.S. citizens working for U.S. companies in foreign countries.

Cases and Exercises

Experiential Exercise: Too Informal? (page 73)

1. **How could the EEOC prove adverse impact?** This could be proven fairly easily by showing that none of the 20 non-Hispanic candidates from the state employment office were hired while Hispanic candidates were. Additionally, they may want to find non-Hispanic candidates who tried to apply but were turned away because the company does not accept walk-in applicants.

2. **Cite specific discriminatory personnel practices at John Jones' company.** By using the "old-boy network" method of recruiting (seeking referrals from current employees), the company prevented non-Hispanics from applying. There was a strong disparate impact.

3. **How could Jones' company defend itself against the allegations of discriminatory practice?** Maybe they could plead ignorance? Jones' best defense may actually be to recognize the deficiency of his company's practices and aggressively seek to formalize its procedures.

4. **Would it make sense for this company to try to defend itself against the discrimination allegations?** It actually may not make sense to try to defend itself. The EEOC is more interested in compliance than in sanctions or punishment. Seeking to change the process to reach compliance may be the best defense against fines or lawsuits.

Case Incident: A Case of Racial Discrimination? (page 74)

1. **What do you think of the way Chapman handled the accusations from Peters in his conversation with Anderson? How would you have handled them?** There is no indication in the case that Chapman asked Peters opinion of what was happening. If that is true, then Chapman may have entered the meeting already having pre-judged Peters. If it were my situation to manage, I might begin by questioning Peters more thoroughly as to the

nature of the notes he received. I would also want to know why Peters had not confronted Anderson directly and asked her to stop.

2. **Do you think Peters had the basis for a sexual harassment claim against Anderson? Why or why not?** If you allow the class time to explore this, the class will likely divide over this issue. An essential element is Peters' lack of confrontation of Anderson. Peters might have had a reasonable claim of harassment had he informed Anderson of his disapproval of her behavior (informality, notes, and calls) and had she then persisted in her actions. At this stage, he appears to have very little legal grounds for harassment.

3. **What would you do now if you were Chapman to avoid further incidence of this type?** I would take a number of steps. First, I would meet with the hospitals attorney to review what happened and get a firm legal opinion. Second, I would make sure that the hospital has a clear written policy and documentation from each employee that they have reviewed the policy. The policy should include a standard procedure for handling this type of problem. Finally, I would want to include this the subject of harassment in orientation and training programs for doctors and staff.

Case Application: All in the Family (page 75)

1. **To what extent did Minardi's vacant position advertisement correspond to the qualifications Louis Minardi was looking for?** Minardi was looking for someone to supervise eight men who were older and who had worked in a bakery 7-10 years. It seems he really preferred someone with bakery experience. The add suggested that either technical training or supervisory experience were sufficient. Minardi wanted someone he was comfortable with and his "men" were comfortable with.

2. **Suggested Question: Why might Takia feel she was discriminated against?** Takia had the requirements noted in the advertisement. In her interview, she may have felt she was not taken seriously (her interview was interrupted several times. Minardi asked her about her boyfriend (which might suggest to her that she needs a man's permission to do her job), he asked her directly about her experience supervising men (sent the message that supervising women was not valid experience for supervising men) and paid little attention to her assertions that she had education in her field (a criteria listed in the job description). The employment application asked questions that did not relate to the job (do you owe money?). The person hired appears to be about her age.

3. **Suggested Question: What could Minardi have done differently that would have reduced the likelihood of having a this type of problem?** Minardi did not appear to have thoughtfully considered the requirements for the position. His advertisement was misleading. He does not appear to have considered the possibility that a woman could accomplish the task. While it does not mention the age of the person hired, he also appears to be young. Minardi would likely have benefited from some professional consultation before he began the hiring process.

Chapter 3
Job Analysis

In Brief: In this chapter, Dessler explains the uses of job analysis information and carefully describes the methods of conducting a job analysis. The tasks of writing job descriptions and job specifications are also outlined. Finally, he discusses the trend of enlarging and de-jobbing positions.

Interesting Issues: There is a tension in today's organizational environment between: a) the desire and need to clearly define jobs and job expectations and b) the trend towards job enlargement and "de-jobbing." The news is filled with examples of companies who have moved towards enlargement of jobs (usually coupled with downsizing). This would be a good point to compare and contrast these demands with the demands and expectations for clear job analysis, design, descriptions, and specifications.

Lecture Outline

I.   **The Nature of Job Analysis**

      A.   Job Analysis Defined

            1.   Job analysis

            2.   Job description

            3.   Job specification

      B.   Uses of Job Analysis Information

            1.   Recruitment and Selection

            2.   Compensation

            3.   Performance Appraisal

            4.   Training

            5.   Ensure Complete Assignment of Duties

      C.   Steps in Job Analysis

            1.   Identify the use to which the information will be put.

            2.   Review relevant background information.

            3.   Select representative positions to be analyzed.

4. Analyze the job by collecting data.

5. Review the information with job incumbents.

6. Develop a job description and job specification.

II. Methods of Collecting Job Analysis Information

A. Introduction

1. Who collects the job information?

2. The information collection process.

B. The Interview

1. Types

   a. individual interviews
   b. group interviews
   c. supervisor interviews

2. Pros and Cons

3. Typical Questions (page 88)

   Figure 3-3 on pages 89-90 gives an example of a job questionnaire.

4. Interview Guidelines

C. Questionnaires

D. Observation

E. Participant Diary / Logs

F. U.S. Civil Service Procedure

Figure 3-4 on page 93 shows a sample Civil Service Job Analysis Record Sheet.

G. Quantitative Job Analysis Techniques

1. Position Analysis Questionnaire (PAQ)

   Figure 3-5 on page 95 shows a sample portion of a PAQ.

2. Department of Labor Procedure

   Table 3-1 on page 96 shows a set of basic activities.

Figure 3-6 on page 96 gives a sample summary.

4.   Functional job analysis

H.   Getting Multiple Perspectives is Advisable.

III. Writing Job Descriptions

Information Technology and HR box on page 97 describes internet-accessible job descriptions.

Figure 3-8 on page 100 gives a sample job description.

A.   Job Identification

B.   Job Summary

C.   Relationships

D.   Responsibilities and Duties

E.   Standards of Performance

F.   Working Conditions and Physical Environment

G.   Job Description Guidelines

1.   Writing job descriptions that comply with the ADA.

2.   Identifying essential job functions.

H.   Small Business Applications: A Practical Job Analysis Approach

page 103 of text; see Discussion Boxes solution at end of this chapter.

IV.   Writing Job Specifications

A.   Specifications for Trained Versus Untrained Personnel

B.   Job Specifications Based on Judgment

C.   Job Specifications Based on Statistical Analysis

V.   Job Analysis in a "Jobless" World

A.   Introduction

B.   From Specialized to Enlarged Jobs

    C.   Why Companies are Becoming De-jobbed: The Need for Competitiveness

        1.   Flatter organizations

        2.   Work teams

        3.   The boundaryless organizations

        4.   Reengineering

        5.   The future of job descriptions

    D.   The High-Performance Organization: Modern Job Analysis Methods

        page 112 of text; see Discussion Boxes solutions at end of this chapter

        1.   The Skills Matrix (Figure 3-13, page 113)

Discussion Boxes

Small Business Applications: A Practical Job Analysis Approach
(pages 103-107)

      This dialogue box discusses the difficulties that an HR manager or business owner has in a small organization. Without the many resources of a large organization, how do they accomplish the tasks of job analysis? This treatment gives a step-by-step guide for the manager in this situation. You may want to use this opportunity to discuss the differences between large and small organizations as related to job analysis tasks.

The High Performance Organization: Modern Job Analysis Methods
(pages 112-113)

      There are a growing number of firms that are shifting to HR systems that don't use job descriptions. So what replaces them? This discussion examines what British Petroleum's Exploration Division has done. they use a matrix of skills and skill levels. The major purpose was to shift employees from thinking in terms of "it's not my job" to thinking about what new skills they needed to accomplish their goals.

This interesting shift should be one that could generate discussion in the class. Ask class members questions such as:
          "So how do you know if you are doing your job?"
          "How would performance appraisals be done?"
          "How do you ensure fairness between employees?"
          "As a supervisor, how do you keep your employee doing what he or she should?"

Key Terms
---

job analysis	The procedure for determining the duties and skill requirements of a job and the kind of person who should be hired for it. (page 84)
job description	A list of a job's duties, responsibilities, reporting relationships, working conditions, and supervisory responsibilities--one product of a job analysis. (page 84)
job specification	A list of a job's "human requirements," that is, the requisite education, skills, personality, and so on--another product of a job analysis. (page 84)
diary/log	Daily listings made by workers of every activity in which they engage along with the time each activity takes. (page 92)
position analysis questionnaire (PAQ)	A questionnaire used to collect quantifiable data concerning the duties and responsibilities of various jobs. (page 94)
Department of Labor job analysis	Standardized method for rating, classifying, and comparing virtually every kind of job based on data, people, and things. (page 94)
functional job analysis	A method for classifying jobs similar to the Department of Labor job analysis but additionally taking into account the extent to which instructions, reasoning, judgment, and verbal facility are necessary for performing the job tasks. (page 97)

Discussion Questions:
---

1. **What items are typically included in the job description? What items are not shown?**
   A job description is a written statement of what the jobholder actually does, how he or she does it, and under what conditions the job is performed. There is no standard format for writing job descriptions, but most descriptions include sections on: (pages 98-103)

   - job identification
   - job summary
   - relationships, responsibilities and duties
   - authority of incumbent
   - standards of performance
   - working conditions
   - job specifications

2. **What is job analysis? How can you make use of the information it provides?** Job analysis is the procedure through which you determine the duties and nature of the jobs and the kinds of people who should be hired for them. You can utilize the information it provides to write job descriptions and job specifications which are utilized in recruitment and selection, compensation, performance appraisal, and training. (pages 84-85)

3. **We discussed several methods for collecting job analysis data—questionnaires, the position analysis questionnaire, and so on. Compare and contrast these methods, explaining what each is useful for and listing the pros and cons of each.** Interviews are probably the most widely used method of collecting information for job analysis. The interview allows the incumbent to report activities that might not otherwise come to light (mental activities and activities that occur only occasionally). Observation is useful for jobs that consist mainly of physical activity that is clearly observable. Questionnaires are a quick and efficient way of obtaining information from a large number of employees, however, development cost can be high. Participant diary logs can provide a comprehensive picture of a job, especially when supplemented with interviews, however, many employees do not respond well to the request to record all their daily activities. Quantitative job analysis techniques, such as PAQ, DOL, and Functional Job Analysis, are more appropriate when the aim is to assign a quantitative value to each job so that jobs can be compared for pay purposes. (pages 87-98)

4. **Describe the types of information typically found in a job specification.** It should include a list of the human traits and experience needed to perform the job. These might include education, skills, behaviors, personality traits, work experience, sensory skills, etc. (pages 107-109)

5. **Explain how you would conduct a job analysis.** There are six major steps in a well-conducted job analysis: 1) Determine how the job analysis information will be used and how to collect the necessary information; 2) Collect background information such as organization charts, process charts, and job descriptions; 3) Select representative positions to be analyzed; 4) Collect job analysis information; 5) Review the information with the participants; 6) Develop job descriptions and job specifications. (pages 85-87)

6. **Do you think companies can really do without detailed job descriptions? Why or why not?** Either side is an acceptable position to take. The key to grading this answer is the quality of the "why or why not" explanations. Look for students to clearly explain their position in terms of the effects of the lack of job descriptions on the performance, motivation, and capabilities of the people doing the job.

7. **Since the president's job in a firm is by nature broader than a factory worker's, is there less need for a job description for the president? Why or why not?** It is clearly more difficult to write a job description for a broad position such as president. This does not, however, mean that it is less important. The position a student takes on this question has much to do with whether he or she believes that the purpose of a job description is needed for the position of president. In other words, does the president need to know what is expected of him or her? Does the board need to know what they should evaluate the president's performance on? Or, does their need to be a job description so that if the position is open, there is appropriate information to advertise with? Look for sound arguments and reasoning.

Individual and Group Activities:

1. **Working individually or in groups, obtain copies of job descriptions for clerical positions at the college or university where you study, or the firm where you work. What types of information do they contain? Do they give you enough information to explain what the job involves and how to do it? How would you improve on the descriptions?** Based on our experience, it is very likely that at least some of the job descriptions will not contain all the information that is supposed to be there. Use this as an opportunity to discuss the problems that may be created by the missing information.

2. **Working individually or in groups, use the job analysis questionnaire in this chapter to develop a job description for your professor in this class. Based on that, use your judgment to develop a job specification. Compare your conclusions with those of other students or groups. Were there any significant differences? What do you think accounted for the differences?** Some significant areas that may prove difficult for the students may include: Relationships, responsibilities, and duties; Authority of incumbent; Standards of performance; Working conditions; and Job specifications. Use this opportunity to help them understand the difficulties in capturing all the aspects of a job that involves judgment, flexibility, and discretion.

3. **Working individually or in groups, obtain a copy of the DOT from your library. Choose any two positions and compare the jobs' DATA-PEOPLE-THINGS ratings. (These are the 4th, 5th, and 6th digits of the job's DOT number; ratings are explained at the end of the DOT). Do the ratings make sense based on what you know about the jobs? Why or why not?** Students may use this opportunity to also find out more about some specific types of jobs in which they may have an interest.

Cases and Exercises:

Experiential Exercise: The Job Description (page 115)

Use this exercise to help students:

- Obtain some hands-on experience with job analysis.
- To gain some understanding that different methods will likely yield different results.

Case Incident: Hurricane Bonnie (page 119)

1. **Should Phil and Linda ignore the old-timers' protests and write up the job descriptions as they see fit? Why? How would you go about resolving the differences?** In all likelihood, the old-timers are accurate in their descriptions. There are several of them, and it appears that all of their descriptions agree. Also, since they were the ones actually doing the work, it is likely that they were the only ones who knew what was

actually being done. One way to resolve the differences would be to examine the specific items that Phil and Maybelline feel the old-timers are padding their jobs with. Ask for evidence from the old-timers that they did these functions, and ask for evidence from Phil and Maybelline that someone else carried out those tasks.

2. **How would you have conducted the job analysis?** Other options may have been to conduct personal interviews instead of the questionnaires. However, it is unlikely that the resulting disagreement would have been avoided by using another method. The method that they used was a good one.

Case Application: Does Your Secretary Rank Higher Than Mine (page 119)

1. **What do you think the problem is from Garrett's point of view?** Garrett has expressed concern that his secretary will be ranked lower than the secretaries of other vice presidents, reducing her secretary. If this happens, he feels his secretary will leave.

2. **How should Elizabeth address each of the concerns expressed?** While wanting to meet Garrett's concerns, Elizabeth must recognize her responsibility is to the company as a whole. She must develop a rational analysis that can support her recommendations.

3. **What can Elizabeth do to prepare herself for any resistance to the analysis from the secretaries themselves?**. Elizabeth needs to inform the secretaries of the true purpose of the survey. Compensation at Dublin should be based on how well employees perform at particular jobs. Over time, it seems the jobs at Dublin have sufficiently changed so that not all secretaries are performing the same level of work. Some secretaries may be underpaid.

4. **Given current advances in office technology such as sophisticated spreadsheet programs, voice mail systems, and e-mail as well as the elimination of many middle-management positions through downsizing, secretaries in many firms are taking on quasi-management tasks. How can Elizabeth account in her job analysis for the many degrees to which individual secretaries at Dublin are doing so?** Elizabeth needs to capture as much information as possible about the 1) technical nature of the work and 2) the work volume. These two dimensions, in addition to her other information, will help her determine the boundaries of jobs (what skills/competencies they contain).

Chapter 4
Personnel Planning and Recruiting

In Brief: This chapter explains the process of forecasting personnel requirements, discusses the pros and cons of eight methods used for recruiting job candidates, describes how to develop an application form, and explains how to use application forms to predict job performance.

Interesting Issues: Despite lots of publicity and widespread knowledge of EEO laws, many organizations still ask questions that are highly suspect, and some questions that are clearly violations of federal regulations. It may be useful to discuss causes of this and the potential consequences of those violations.

Lecture Outline

I.   The Recruitment and Selection Process

      A.   Employment Planning and Forecasting

      B.   Building a Pool of Candidates

      C.   Application Forms and Initial Screening Interview

      D.   Utilizing Various Selection Techniques

      E.   Sending Viable Candidates to the Supervisor

      F.   Conducting Final Selection Interviews

      Figure 4-1 on page 123 outlines the selection process.

II.   Employment Planning and Forecasting

      A.   How to Forecast Personnel Needs

            1.   Factors to consider after sales projections & staff requirements

                  a.   projected turnover
                  b.   quality and nature of employees
                  c.   decisions to upgrade product quality or enter new markets
                  d.   technological and administrative changes
                  e.   financial resources available

            2.   Trend Analysis

            3.   Ratio Analysis

            4.   Scatter Plot

Figure 4-2 on page 125 gives a sample scatter plot.

     5.   Using Computers to Forecast Personnel Requirements

     6.   Managerial Judgment

  B.   Forecasting the Supply of Insider Candidates

     1.   Qualifications Inventories

     2.   Manual Systems and Replacement Charts

         a.   personnel inventory and development record (shown in Figure 4-3 on page 127)
         b.   personnel replacement charts (sample shown in figure 4-4 on page 128)
         c.   position replacement cards

     3.   Computerized Information Systems

     4.   The Matter of Privacy

  C.   Internal Sources of Candidates

     1.   Job Posting

     2.   Hiring Employees—The Second Time Around

     3.   Succession Planning

  D.   Forecasting the Supply of Outside Candidates

     1.   General Economic Conditions

     2.   Local Market Conditions

     3.   Occupational Market Conditions

III.   Recruiting Job Candidates

  A.   Introduction

     1.   Figure 4-6 shows a sample Recruiting Yield Pyramid

     2.   Research Insight

  B.   Advertising as a Source of Candidates

Chapter 4: Personnel Planning and Recruiting

        1.   Principles of Help Wanted Advertising

            a.   attract attention
            b.   develop interest
            c.   create desire
            d.   prompt action

Table 4-2 on page 138 gives advantages and disadvantages of various media.

C.   Employment Agencies as a Source of Candidates

        1.   Types

            a.   Federal, state, or local government operated
            b.   Nonprofit organizations
            c.   Privately owned

        2.   Reasons for Using Employment Agencies

            a.   don't have your own HR department
            b.   past difficulty generating sufficient qualified applicants
            c.   opening must be filled quickly
            d.   perceived need to attract more minority or female applicants
            e.   want to reach those who are currently employed

        3.   Using Temporary Help Agencies

            a.   six concerns with temporary workers
            b.   six guidelines for working with temporary employees

        4.   Alternative Staffing Techniques

D.   Executive Recruiters as a Source of Candidates

        1.   Make Sure the Firm is Capable of Conducting a Thorough Search

        2.   Meet the Individual Who Will be Handling Your Assignment

        3.   Ask How Much the Search Firm Charges

        4.   Choose a Recruiter You Can Trust

        5.   Talk to Some of Their Clients

Small Business Applications:
page 148 of the text; see Discussion Boxes solutions at the end of this chapter

E.   College Recruiting as a Source of Candidates

Table 4-3 on page 151 identifies the top factors in selecting college recruiters.

Table 4-4 on page 151 identifies the top factors in selecting schools to recruit.

F.   Referrals and Walk-Ins as a Source of Candidates

G.   Recruiting on the Internet

Figure 4-14 on page 153 shows an example of recruiting on the internet.

H.   The High-Performance Organization: Recruiting Tech Workers

page 155 of text; see Discussion Boxes solutions at end of this chapter.

I.   Recruiting a More Diverse Work Force

      1.   Older Workers as a Source of Candidates

      2.   Diversity Counts: Recruiting Single Parents

            pages 156-157 of text; see Discussion Boxes solutions

      3.   Recruiting Minorities and Women

      4.   Welfare-to-Work

J.   Some Other Recruiting Sources

K.   Recruiting Methods Used

      1.   Global HRM: The Global Talent Search
            pages 159-160 of text; see Discussion Boxes solutions

IV. Developing and Using Application Forms

A.   Purpose of Application Forms

B.   Equal Opportunity and Application Forms

      1.   Potentially Discriminatory Questions.

      2.   Mandatory Dispute Resolution.

C.   Using Application Forms to Predict Job Performance

      1.   Using Application Forms to Predict Job Tenure

      2.   Using Application Forms to Predict Employee Theft

Discussion Boxes

Building Employee Commitment: Promotion From Within
(page 130)

This dialogue box discusses the employee commitment that promotion from within opportunities create. It also takes the time to discuss factors that make a promotion from within policy work. These factors include careful employee selection, education and training, career-oriented appraisals, systems for accessing career records, and posting of job openings.

This dialogue box can be used to generate discussion on the impacts of promotion from within on the students' own attitudes and commitment as well as the complexities of making such a system really work.

Small Business Applications
(pages 148-149)

This dialogue box talks about the reasons a small business might want to consider using an executive recruiting firm in spite of the seemingly high costs associated with such organizations. This could certainly be used to help students consider the lost opportunity costs involved with some activities, as well as how much the tangible costs of doing an executive search really will add up to. It might be helpful to have examples of what display advertisements in large city newspapers and professional journals cost. Have them consider how large an ad might need to be to be successful, and how many times it might need to run.

The High-Performance Organization: Recruiting Tech Workers
(page 155)

Turnover among high-tech workers is reportedly around 17% and about 1 out of 10 information technology jobs is going empty. This dialogue box explains how one company, GE Medical Systems, has approached the problem. The focus of GE Medical has been on internal processes. They have borrowed extensively from their benchmarking of suppliers and from their manufacturing planning to measure their personnel processes and forecast their personnel needs.

Diversity Counts: Recruiting Single Parents
(pages 156-157)

This dialogue box discusses several issues surrounding the single parent, and especially the single mother in the workforce. As this is a significant part of today's population, it is important that students understand the issues and problems facing these individuals. It might be useful to have a discussion about the issues and to brainstorm for additional ways to make the workplace "single-parent friendly."

Global HRM: The Global Talent Search (page 154)

Human Resource Management

This dialogue box discusses the efforts of companies to recruit foreign nationals in order to staff their expanding overseas operations. Use this to generate discussion on the advantages of having local nationals in management of foreign locations versus sending Americans to those locations. You may want to discuss some of the legal restrictions on using Americans in many foreign countries. Also consider a discussion on the difficulties of recruiting in another culture.

Key Terms

trend analysis	Study of a firm's past employment needs over a period of years to predict future needs. (page 124)
ratio analysis	A forecasting technique for determining future staff needs by using ratios between sales volume and number of employees needed. (page 124)
scatter plot	A graphical method used to help identify the relationship between two variables. (page 125)
computerized forecast	The determination of future staff needs by projecting a firm's sales, volume of production, and personnel required to maintain this volume of output, using computers and software packages. (page 126)
qualifications inventories	Manual or computerized systematic records, listing employees' education, career and development interests, languages, special skills, and so on, to be used in forecasting inside candidates for promotion. (page 126)
personnel replacement charts	Company records showing present performance and promotability of inside candidates for the most important positions. (page 126)
position replacement cards	A card prepared for each position in a company to show possible replacement candidates and their qualifications. (page 126)
job posting	Posting notices of job openings on company bulletin boards is an effective recruiting method. (page 131)
occupational market conditions	The Bureau of Labor Statistics of the U.S. Department of Labor publishes projections of labor supply and demand for various occupations, as do other agencies. (page 133)
application form	The form that provides information on education, prior work record, and skills. (page 160)

Discussion Questions:

1. **Compare and contrast five sources of job candidates.** The text lists several sources of job candidates, both internal and external. The student should clearly identify the differences as well as comparative strengths and weaknesses of each. There are at least the following sources to choose from: advertising, employment agencies, executive recruiters, state job services, college recruiting, referrals, employee database, internal, and talent searches (pages 132 - 154).

2. **What types of information can an application form provide?** The application form is a good means of quickly collecting verifiable, and therefore potentially accurate, historical data from the candidate. It usually includes information on education, prior work history, and other experience related to the job The application form can provide four types of information: 1. substantive matters (such as education and experience); 2. applicant's previous progress and growth; 3. stability based on previous work history; 4. prediction of job success. (page 154)

3. **Discuss how equal employment laws apply to personnel planning and recruiting activities.** The student should be able to discuss the areas in which the laws and regulations covered in Chapter 2 apply to the issues of planning and recruiting. This would include constraints on sources used for candidates (i.e. not excessive reliance on referrals), the wording of questions asked on application forms or in interviews, and planning decisions that must not be overly detrimental to a protected group.

Individual and Group Activities:

1. **Working individually or in groups, develop an application form for the position of supervisor of Marketing Manager as described in the sample job description in Figure 3-8, Chapter 3. Compare the application forms produced by different individuals or groups. Are there any items that should be dropped due to EEO restrictions? Are there any items you would add to make your application form more complete?** Be sure to watch for EEO issues; are all the questions legal or are any questionable? Also, do the questions seek the appropriate information that is relevant to this type of position. Some information that should be included might be: experience, education, training, and organizations.

2. **Working individually or in groups, bring to class several classified and display ads from this Sunday's help wanted ads. Analyze the effectiveness of these ads using the guidelines discussed in this chapter.** The effectiveness should be analyzed using the list on page 136 which includes: attracts attention, develops interest, creates desire, and prompts action.

3. **Working individually or in groups, obtain a recent copy of the *Monthly Labor Review* or *Occupational Outlook Quarterly,* both published by the U.S. Bureau of Labor Statistics. Based on information in either of these publications, develop a forecast for the next five years of occupational market conditions for various occupations such as accountant, nurse, and engineer.** Be sure that the forecasts that the students develop are grounded in information gleaned from these sources. They should have an adequate analysis of the statistics.

4. **Working individually or in groups, visit your local office of your state employment agency. Come back to class prepared to discuss the following questions: What types of jobs seemed to be available through this agency, predominantly? To what extent do you think this particular agency would be a good source of professional, technical, and/or managerial applicants? What sort of paperwork are applicants to the state agency required to complete before their applications are processed by the agency? What other opinions did you form about the state agency?** The answers to this will vary greatly by state and local offices. Generally, these agencies may be more oriented to unskilled and skilled position, rarely do they handle much professional and managerial position...although some do quite a bit. Although students may come back with a negative view of these offices, help them to understand the valuable role that they do play. A special note of courtesy: make sure that your have discussed this assignment with the local agency office. Surprise visits by several groups during busy periods can create some especially negative relations between the office and your school. Make sure they are welcome and expected.

5. **Working individually or in groups, review help wanted ads placed over the last few Sundays by local employment agencies. Do some employment agencies seem to specialize in some types of jobs? If you were an HR manager seeking a relationship with an employment agency for each of the following types of jobs, which local agencies would you turn to first, based on their help wanted ad history: engineers, secretaries, data processing clerks, accountants, factory workers?** Help the students to relate this exercise to the earlier one on evaluating the effectiveness of advertisements. To what extent are their perceptions a result of good advertising? To what extent may these perceptions be accurate or not? What other information might they want before actually contracting with an agency? (pages 136-145)

6. **Working individually or in groups, interview an HR manager to determine the specific actions his or her company is taking to recruit a more diverse workforce. Back in class, compare the activities of the different employers.** There should be some differences, but mostly similarities, between the managers. Discuss the differences and possible reasons for those differences. Some reasons may include the difficulties (or lack of) in recruiting a diverse workforce in their industry or area, the commitment of the company towards a diverse workforce, etc.

Cases and Exercises:

Experiential Exercise: Forecasting Personnel Requirements (pages 166-167)

1. **Based on the admittance trends, what number of nurses do you estimate Park General Hospital will need over the next 2 years?** Next year = 625. Year after next = 636.

2. **Based on turnover forecasts, how many nurses do you estimate Park General Hospital will need to replace in the next 2 years?** Total for next year should be 65 and the following year should be 70.

3. **Given your answers to items 1 and 2, how many nurses does your department need to recruit?** The charts are not entirely clear about the current number of nurses employed. The admittance trends chart seems to skip the current year. This may throw off some students. However, they should use trend analysis to conclude that there are most likely 620 nurses currently. Based on this, the needs will be:
   Next year: 625 - 620 + 65 = 70
   Year after next: 636 – 625 + 70 = 81

Case Incident: A Tight Labor Market for Cleaners (page 167)

1. **Provide a detailed list of recommendations concerning yow Jennifer should go about increasing the number of acceptable job applicants so that her company need no longer hire "just about anyone" who walks in the door. Specifically, your recommendations should include:**

   a. **Completely worded classified ads.** Students will vary in their creative approaches. A good teaching method is to have them email their ads to each other and have the students rank order which ad they would apply to. Determine what made the ad attractive and ask the other students to modify the ad according to what they just learned.

   b. **Recommendations concerning any other recruiting strategies you suggest they use.** Students will offer a wide variety of suggestions. Among the likely responses are: radio ads, flyers/handbills, and direct mail to former employees (we miss you—maybe the grass didn't turn out to be greener on the other side). Some students will consider target marketing. For example, Jennifer could re-engineer the job to fewer hours and recruit part time workers, greatly increasing the pool of potential employees.

2. **What practical suggestions could you make that might help reduce turnover and make the stores a more attractive place in which to work (thereby reducing recruiting problems)?** Jennifer can do a quick analysis on what it costs her to recruit and train a new employee (including the cost of lower productivity as a person learns a new job). Every reduction in employee turnover can be translated to dollars. In fact, Jennifer can improve working conditions without any change in her profit if she pays for improvements from

savings in employee turnover costs. The best source of ideas from improvement may come from exit interviews (what would we have done to our work environment that would have made you more likely to stay?), and from existing employees. Students are also likely to suggest some of the following; air-conditioned work space, more employees (so workers work fewer hours), longer or more frequent breaks. Other students will consider more complicate solutions like job rotation. Still others might suggest the use of deferred compensation or profit sharing to keep employees a full year (e.g., $8.50 per hour, $7.50 now, one dollar per hour paid at year end to the remaining employees).

Case Application: Finding People Who Are Passionate About What They Do
(page 168)

Trilogy Software is a fast growing software company with a unique and highly unorthodox culture. The case provides a framework for discussing issues related to person company fit and the role of recruiting in that process.

1. **Identify some of the established selection techniques that underlie Trilogy's unconventional approach to hiring?** Trilogy actively recruits potential employees early in the hiring cycle. Their techniques include reviewing resumes (over 15,000 in one year), attending job and career fairs, conducting on campus interviews (over 4,000), flying in prospects for interviews, and having more personalized procedures for handling top recruits.

2. **What particular elements of Trilogy's culture most likely appeal to the kind of employees it seeks? How does it convey those elements to job prospects?** A number of company characteristics many appeal to programmers, including: no dress code, no regular work schedule, self-directed scheduling, workers with similar interests and technically challenging work.

3. **Would Trilogy be an appealing employer for you? Why or why not? If not, what would it take for you to accept a job offer from Trilogy?** Students may answer this either way. Students who require more structure may want to know about career paths, mentoring and measures of success. They may want the company to make some sort of symbolic comment to them.

Chapter 5
Employee Testing and Selection

In Brief: This chapter gives an overview of the selection process, testing concepts, types of tests, and selection techniques. It also addresses legal and ethical questions surrounding the area of testing and selection.

Interesting Issues: Most companies desire reference and background information to make employment decisions, however, most companies also have policies against giving out any information on current or past employees beyond basic job titles and dates of employement. Students need to see the tug-of-war between privacy rights and employer needs for background and predictive information.

Lecture Outline

I. **The Selection Process**

    A.   Why the Careful Selection is Important

        1.   Performance

        2.   Costs

        3.   Legal Implications and Negligent Hiring

II. **Basic Testing Concepts**

    A.   Validity

        1.   Criterion Validity

        2.   Content Validity

    B.   Reliability

        1.   Retest Estimate

        2.   Equivalent Form Estimate

        3.   Internal Consistency

    C.   Sources of Unreliability

        1.   Poor Sampling of the Material

2. Chance Response Tendencies

3. Testing Conditions

4. Changes in the Person

D. How to Validate a Test

   1. Analyze the Job

   2. Choose your Tests

   3. Administer the Test

      a. concurrent validation
      b. predictive validation

   4. Relate Test Scores and Criteria

      Figure 5-3 on page 178 shows a sample expectancy chart.

   5. Cross-validation and Revalidation

E. Testing Guidelines

   1. Use Tests as Supplements

   2. Validate the Tests

   3. Analyze All your Current Hiring and Promotion Standards

   4. Keep Accurate Records

   5. Begin your Validation Program Now

   6. Use a Certified Psychologist

   7. Test Conditions are Important

III. **Ethical and Legal Questions in Testing**

A. Equal Employment Opportunity Implications

   1. Your Alternatives

      a. choose and alternative selection procedure
      b. show that the test is valid
      c. monitor the selection test to see if it has disparate impact

Chapter 5: Employee Testing and Selection

        2.   Individual Rights of Test Takers and Test Security

        3.   Research Insight

        4.   The Issue of Privacy

    B.   Using Tests at Work

IV.   Types of Tests

    A.   Tests of Cognitive Abilities

        1.   Intelligence Tests

        2.   Specific Cognitive Abilities (aptitude)

    B.   Tests of Motor and Physical Abilities

    C.   Measuring Personality and Interests

        1.   Projective Personality Tests

        2.   Interest Inventories

    D.   Achievement Tests

Information Technology & HR: Computers--Interactive Performance Test, page 183 of the text: This dialogue box discusses the use of computers in measuring performance.

V.   Work Samples and Simulations

    A.   Work Sampling for Employee Selection

    B.   Developing a Work Sampling Procedure

    C.   Management Assessment Centers

        1.   Assessment Centers in Practice

    D.   Video-Based Situational Testing

    E.   The Miniature Job Training and Evaluation Approach

    F.   The High-Performance Organization: Skills Testing
          pages 189-190 of the text. See discussion boxes solution at end of this chapter.

VI. **Other Selection Techniques**

    A.   Background Investigations and Reference Checks

        1.   Use

        2.   Effectiveness

        3.   Giving Employment References: Know the Law

        4.   Making Background and Reference Checks More Useful

        5.   Preemployment Information Services

    B.   The Polygraph and Honesty Testing

        1.   Strict limits on use of Polygraph

        2.   Paper-and-Pencil Tests

        3.   A Caution

    C.   Graphology

    D.   Physical Examination

    E.   Drug Screening

    F.   Testing, Selection, and Organizational Performance

    G.   Complying with the Immigration Law

    G.   Small Business Applications: Testing and Reference Checking

        pages 204-206 of the text: see Discussion Boxes solutions at end of this chapter

Discussion Boxes

The High-Performance Organization: Skills Testing
(pages 189-190)

    This dialogue box describes the assessment/training program developed by Texas Instruments Semiconductor Group. In addition to doing evaluation, they also provide on-site training programs to give employees the specific skills that they test for in the assessment center.

Small Business Applications: Testing and Reference Checking
(pages 204-206)

This dialogue box discusses the potential use of testing in small businesses as well as the implications of reference checking and giving policies. Key points:

Testing
- Important and critical for small business
- Wonderlic Personnel Test
- Predictive Index
- Minnesota Clerical Assessment Battery

Reference Checking Policies
- Should seek them
- Fewer problems with tardiness, absenteeism, work quality

Reference Giving Policies
- One third of all slander & libel cases were by former employees against employer
- 77% of these cases won by employee
- Only one person should give references
- Limit reference information to dates, salary, title, and superior
- Base references only on facts
- Give references only with signed release by employee
- Avoid verbal references

Key Terms

test validity	The accuracy with which a test, interview, and so on measures what it purports to measure or fulfills the function it was designed to fill. (page 174)
criterion validity	A type of validity based on showing that scores on the test (predictors) are related to job performance. (page 174)
content validity	A test that is content--valid is one in which the test contains a fair sample of the tasks and skills actually needed for the job in question. (page 175)
reliability	The characteristic which refers to the consistency of scores obtained by the same person when retested with the identical or equivalent tests. (page 175)
expectancy chart	A graph showing the relationship between test scores and job performance for a large group of people. (page 178)

work samples	Actual job tasks used in testing applicants' performance. (page 186)
work sampling technique	A testing method based on measuring performance on actual job tasks. (page 186)
management assessment centers	A situation in which management candidates are asked to make decisions in hypothetical situations and are scored on their performance. It usually also involves testing and the use of management games. (page 187)

Discussion Questions:

1. **Explain what is meant by reliability and validity. What is the difference between them? In what respects are they similar?** Reliability is the consistency of scores obtained by the same persons when retested with identical tests or with an equivalent form of a test. It is a measure of internal consistency of the instrument. Validity is the degree to which a test measures what it is purported to measure. It is a measure of external consistency. They are similar in that both are concerned with aspects of consistency of the instrument, and that reliability is a necessary condition for validity. (pages 174-175)

2. **Explain how you would go about validating a test. How can this information be useful to a manager?** The validation process consists of five steps: job analysis, selecting a test, administering a test, relating the test scores and the criteria, and cross validation and revalidation. Using valid selection devices will enable the manager to develop objective information in the selection process and should result in more effective selection decisions. (pages 176-178)

3. **Explain why you think a certified psychologist who is specially trained in test construction should (or should not) always be used by a company developing a personnel test battery.** Due to the complex and legal nature of this activity, the use of a certified psychologist may be the only safe way to accomplish your objectives. However, because of the high salary and limited job scope of such a specialist, a definite drawback to this approach is the cost involved. Perhaps more "direct" tests can be developed which require less sophistication: motor and physical abilities tests (many state employment agencies provide this service), on-job knowledge tests, and work sampling. (pages 179)

4. **Explain how you would use work sampling for employee selection.** The work sampling technique is based on the assumption that the best indicator of future performance is past performance. Here you use the applicant's actual performance on the same (or very similar) job to predict his or her future job performance. The specific tasks in developing a work sampling procedure are spelled out on page 187. (pages 186-187)

5. **Give some examples of how interest inventories could be used to improve employee selection. In doing so, suggest several examples of occupational interests that you believe might predict success in various occupations including college professor, accountant, and computer programmer.** Interest inventories can improve employee

selection by identifying individuals with similar interests to those reported by a substantial percentage of successful incumbents in an occupation. This should clearly increase the likelihood that the applicants will be successful in their new jobs. Interests that one might expect: *accountant:* math, reading, music; *college professor:* public speaking, teaching, counseling; *computer programmer:* math, music, computers. (pages 184-186)

6. **Why is it important to conduct pre-employment background investigations? How would you go about doing so?** Past behavior is the best predictor of future behavior. It is important to gain as much information as possible about past behavior to understand what kinds of behavior one can expect in the future. Knowledge about attendance problems, insubordination issues, theft, or other behavioral problems can certainly help one avoid hiring someone who is likely to repeat those behaviors. Page 196 has some excellent guidelines for background checks. (pages 190-196)

7. **Explain how you would get around the problem of former employers being un-willing to give bad references on their former employees?** Since many companies have strict policies regarding the release of information about former employees, it may not be possible to get information at all, good or bad. However, conducting a thorough reference audit by contacting at least two superiors, two peers, and two subordinates will help increase the chance that you will find someone who is willing to give you the information you need. Also, making the contacts by phone rather than in writing will increase their belief that the information may not be traced back to them. Using the additional technique of asking references for the name of someone else who might be familiar with the applicant's performance will also increase the possibility of getting more information. (pages 193-194)

Individual and Group Activities:

1. **Write a short essay discussing some of the ethical and legal considerations in testing.** State and federal laws, EEOC guidelines, and court decisions require that you must be able to prove that your tests are related to success or failure on the job and that they are not having an adverse impact on members of a protected group. Test takers also have certain basic rights to privacy and information. The test taker also has the right to expect that the test is equally fair to all test takers. (pages 179-182)

2. **Working individually or in groups, develop a test for the Marketing Manager job description that was presented in Chapter 3, Figure 3-8.** Any of the tests mentioned in the book could be developed for this assignment. The questions or information gathered by the test should be information that could clearly be content or criterion validated.

3. **Working individually or in groups, contact the publisher of a standardized test such as the Scholastic Assessment Test and obtain from them written information regarding the test's validity and reliability. Present a short report in class discussing what the test is supposed to measure and the degree to which you think the test does what it is supposed to do, based on the reported validity and reliability scores.** Encourage students to contact different sources; it may be a good idea to have a sign-up sheet so that no two students or groups are gathering information on the same instruments. Students should be able to clearly relate validity and reliability scores to effectiveness.

Cases and Exercises:

Experiential Exercise: The Reference Check (page 208)

1. **What are the most important issues raised by this inquiry?** The most important issue to the employer is the risk of a lawsuit. Even if you provide information and are careful and document everything, the former employee might choose to sue. Suppose you have been careful and win the suit, defending the suit has cost you money and a considerable amount of time. For this reason, many employers limit the information that they provide to the bare basics: dates of employment and job titles. Standing on principle over the right to give specific information about a <u>former</u> employee is hardly worth the effort, nor the expense.

2. **How should the HR manager respond to this inquiry?** The HR manager should already have in place specific guidelines and policies about what kinds of information will be released to a reference check and what will not. If those policies are not in place, they need to be developed and put in place before answering anything more than question #1. If the policies are in place, follow the policies. Suggested policies would include only providing dates of employment and job title. With written permission of the employee, one might provide salary information. Beyond those issues, there is a legal risk.

Case Incident: The Tough Screener (page 209)

1. **What specific legal problems do you think Rosen can run into as a result of his firm's current screening methods? What steps would you suggest he take to eliminate these problems?** There are a couple of specific problems with what Rosen is doing. First, he will need to conduct a validity study of the honesty test and make sure that it is useful and that it does what it says it does.

   There are three problems with the credit check: First, he needs to get the applicant's permission for the check and allow her to see the results, if she desires. Second, he needs to demonstrate the business necessity of such a check, and third, he needs to conduct a study to assure that it is not having an adverse impact. Screening out candidates based on workers' compensation claims is, most likely, completely illegal. Discriminating against those with driving violations are also very questionable, unless he can demonstrate a business-related reason for it.

2. **Given what you know about Rosen's business, write a two-page proposal describing an employee testing and selection program that you would recommend for his firm. Say a few words about the sorts of tests, if any, you would recommend and the application blank questions you would ask, as well as other methods including drug screening and reference checking.** There are some very specific things Rosen is doing that should be kept: The strong reference checking process is very good. Any of the items from the previous question that pass the business necessity tests mentioned, or are determined to be valid and without adverse impact, should be used as well. Additional information that should be gathered includes educational and any financial planning certifications. Given the nature of his business, it might be wise for Rosen to use only

Certified Financial Planners. He may also want to enlist the services of a bonding company to bond his employees since they will have access to confidential information about his clients.

Case Application: Carter Cleaning Company (page 210)

Jennifer and her father are considering methods for screening applicants for their dry cleaning business. In particular, the Carter management team is considering honesty tests, especially for employees who handle cash.

1. **What would be the advantages and disadvantages to Jennifer's company of routinely administering honest tests to all its employees?** Polygraph testing raises a large number of legal and moral issues; issues Carter Cleaning would best avoid. Use some of the available "paper and pencil" honesty tests may be a possibility. In general, these have been shown to be reasonably reliable and valid. They are still controversial. The costs associated with these tests may also make them prohibitive to a small operation like Jennifer's.

2. **Specifically, what other screening techniques could the company use to screen out theft-prone employees? How exactly could these techniques be used?** More thorough make background checks are a recommend technique to eliminate potential thieves. Some firms chose to contract this out to a private security agency (Cost may be an issue to Jennifer. However, the company can quickly check to see if savings from reduced theft would offset the cost of an outside agency. As part of the job preview, Carter must communicate that jobs in her company are worth keeping; dishonesty and theft will not be tolerated. Further company policies regarding theft should be clearly communicated to new and existing employees.

3. **How should her company terminate employees caught stealing and what kind of procedure should be set up for handling reference calls about these employees when they go to other companies looking for jobs?** Terminating employees for theft should include the involvement of proper authorities and should only be done when there is absolute proof of the theft and who committed it. Such an action will also send a message to the other employees that you will not tolerate theft of company resources. While many employers are reluctant to prosecute employees for theft , developing evidence with police and through the courts can be beneficial in providing future employers of the individual with truthful and factual information.

Chapter 6
Interviewing Candidates

In Brief: This chapter gives an overview of types of interviews and their features. It discusses common mistakes in interviewing, and outlines effective interviewing techniques.

Interesting Issues: While structured interviews have been shown to be more valid than non-structured ones, managers tend to resist structured interviews in favor of trusting their own skills as an interviewer.

Lecture Outline

I. **Introduction: Basic Features of Interviews**

    A.   Types of Interviews

        1.   Structured vs Unstructured Interviews

            a.   unstructured or nondirective interviews
            b.   structured or directive interviews

        2.   The Purpose of the Interview

            a.   stress interview
            b.   appraisal interview

        3.   The Interview's Content: The Types of Questions

            a.   situational interview
            b.   job-related interview
            c.   behavioral interview
            d.   psychological interview

        4.   Administering the Interview

            a.   sequential interview
                i.   structured
                ii.   unstructured
            b.   panel interview
            c.   computerized interviews

    B.   How Useful Are Interviews?

    C.   Interviewing and the Law: Employment Discrimination "Testers"

    D.   Information Technology and HR: The Computer-Aided Interview

        page 223 of the text: see Discussion Boxes solutions at end of this chapter

Chapter 6: Interviewing Candidates

II.   What Factors Can Undermine An Interview's Usefulness?

      A.   Snap Judgments

      B.   Negative Emphasis

      C.   Misunderstanding the Job

      D.   Pressure to Hire

      E.   Candidate-Order (Contrast) Error

      F.   Influence of Nonverbal Behavior

      G.   Diversity Counts: Dressing for the Interview

             page 227 of the text: see Discussion Boxes solutions at end of this chapter

      H.   Telegraphing

      I.   Too Much / Too Little Talking

      J.   Playing District Attorney or Psychologist

III.   Designing and Conducting the Effective Interview

      A.   The Structured Interview

           1.   Step 1: Job Analysis

           2.   Step 2: Evaluate the Job Duty Information

           3.   Step 3: Develop Interview Questions

           4.   Step 4: Develop Benchmark Answers

           5.   Step 5: Appoint Interview Panel and Implement

      B.   Guidelines for Conducting an Interview

           1.   Structure the Interview

           2.   Plan the Interview

           2.   Establish Rapport

           3.   Ask Questions

4. Close the Interview

5. Review the Interview

6. Small Business Applications

    page 235 of the text: see Discussion Boxes solutions—end of this chapter

7. The High-Performance Organization: A Total Selection Program

    page 236 of the text: see Discussion Boxes solutions—end of this chapter

Discussion Boxes

Information Technology and HR:
Computer Applications in Interviewing: The Computer-Aided Interview
(page 223)

This dialogue box gives an example of a bank that is using the computer-aided interview. It describes the computer interview and ends by telling us that candidates who were hired by the program were 26% less likely to quit or be fired within 90 days of hiring. Key points:
- The computer program gives candidates a taste of what the job is really like.
- Candidates must handle realistic job situations.
- Hiring officials can review the candidate's performance at their convenience.

Diversity Counts: Dressing for the Interview
(page 227)

This discussion box describes one study which found that the more masculine a woman's dress, the more likely she was to be hired...to a point. If she crossed over the line to being "too masculine" she would be turned down. Good discussions could be generated from this study regarding the "double-standard" that many women face in employment as well as the influence of non-job performance related issues on the acceptability of candidates.

Small Business Applications
(pages 235-236)

A good outline for interviewing candidates for a position at a small business is given in this section. It might be a good discussion point to talk about what the barriers to carrying out this plan would be for small business people. Would they view it as too much work and too complicated? What are the potential costs if they do not utilize the system?

The High-Performance Organization
(pages 236-238)

This discussion box describes Toyota's "Total Selection Program." Figure 6-5 on page 237 gives a summary of the process. A key item is that the system selects not just for skills, but for values. It is a complex, comprehensive process that involves a great deal of time and energy commitment to carry out. Students may want to discuss why other company's may not want to make this commitment. Why does Toyota make the commitment?

Key Terms

nondirective interview	An unstructured conversational-style interview. The interviewer pursues points of interest as they come up in response to questions. (page 216)
directive interview	An interview following a set sequence of questions. (page 216)
stress interview	An interview in which the applicant is made uncomfortable by a series of often rude questions. This technique helps identify hypersensitive applicants and those with low or high stress tolerance. (page 220)
appraisal interview	A discussion following a performance appraisal in which supervisor and employee discuss the employee's rating and possible remedial actions. (page 220)
situational interview	A series of job-related questions which focuses on how the candidate would behave in a given situation. (page 220)
job related interview	A series of job-related questions which focuses on relevant past job-related behaviors. (page 220)
structured sequential interview	An interview in which the applicant is interviewed sequentially by several supervisors and each rates the applicant on a standard form. (page 221)
panel interview	An interview in which a group of interviewers questions the applicant. (page 221)
candidate-order error	An error of judgment on the part of the interviewer due to interviewing one or more very good or very bad candidates just before the interview in question. (page 226)

Discussion Questions:

1. **Explain the four basic ways in which interviews can be classified.** Interviews can be classified according to: (1) degree of structure. This is the extent to which interviews are, or are not, structure with previously designed questions so that each candidate must answer the same things. (2) purpose. Interviews may be designed to accomplish several purposes, including selection, performance appraisal feedback, etc. (3) content. The content of the questions may be situational, job-related, or psychological. (4) the way the interview is administered. Interviews might be conducted by a panel of interviewers, sequentially or all at once, computerized, or personally. (page 216)

2. **Briefly describe each of the following possible types of interviews: unstructured panel interviews; structured sequential interviews; job-related structured interviews.** In the unstructured panel interview, the panel of interviewers asks questions as they come to mind. They do not have a list of questions or points that need to be covered, but may follow many different directions. The structured sequential interview consists of the candidate interviewing one by one with several different interviewers. Each interviewer conducts a structured interview which consists of pre-determined questions and a structured evaluation form to complete. The job-related structured interview consists of pre-determined questions, all of which are designed to asses the applicant's past behaviors for job-related information. (pages 220-222)

3. **For What sorts of jobs do you think computerized interviews are most appropriate? Why?** The computerized interview can be used as a screening device for virtually any type of position which may generate a large number of applicants. It is less likely to be used for managerial positions. However, if there are large numbers of applicants, it could certainly be just a useful there as in skilled, professional, and unskilled positions. (page 222)

4. **Why do you think ". . . situational interviews yield a higher mean validity than do job related or behavioral interviews, which in turn yield a higher mean validity than do psychological interviews?"** The situational interview allows the candidate to answer situational questions based on past experiences in which he or she might have made mistakes, but learned from them. The job-related (or behavioral) interview focuses primarily on past situations, but does not allow for changes in the candidate due to the lessons that he or she might have learned from those experiences. The psychological interview tends to be more speculative regarding traits which are difficult to really measure. (pages 220-221)

5. **Similarly, how do you explain the fact that structured interviews, regardless of content, are more valid than unstructured interviews for predicting job performance?** The structured interview helps to keep the interviewer focused on the types of behaviors, traits, or answers that are desired and have been determined to be predictors of job performance. Unstructured interviews allow interviewers to become sidetracked with things like common interests and other items that are not predictors of job success. (page 219)

6. **Briefly discuss and give examples of at least five common interviewing mistakes. What recommendations would you give for avoiding these interviewing mistakes?**

Chapter 6: Interviewing Candidates

- *Snap Judgments*: This is where the interviewer jumps to a conclusion about the candidate during the first few minutes of the interview. Using a structured interview is one way to help avoid this, as well as training of the interviewers. (page 224)

- *Negative Emphasis*: When an interviewer has received negative information about the candidate, through references or other sources, he or she will almost always view the candidate negatively. The best way to avoid this is to keep references or other information from the interviewer. If possible, have different people do the reference checks and the interviews and not share the information until afterwards. (page 225)

- *Misunderstanding the Job*: When interviewers do not have a good understanding of the job requirements, they do not make good selections of candidates. All interviewers should clearly understand the jobs and know what is needed for success in those jobs. (page 225)

- *Pressure to Hire*: Anytime an interviewer is told that they must hire a certain number of people within a short time frame, poor selection decisions may be made. This type of pressure should be avoided whenever possible. (page 226)

- *Candidate-Order (Contrast) Error*: When an adequate candidate is preceded by either an outstanding, or a poor candidate, by contrast he or she looks either less satisfactory or much better. This can be countered through interviewer training, allowing time between interviews, and structured interviews with structured rating forms. (page 226)

- *Influence of Nonverbal Behavior*: Candidates who exhibit stronger non-verbal behavior such as eye contact and energy level are perceived as stronger by the interviewers. This can be minimized through interviewer training and structured interviews. (page 226)

- *Telegraphing*: An interviewer might "give" the right answers to candidates they hope to hire. This can be combated through structured interview questions, multiple interviewers, and interviewer training. (page 228)

- *Too Much / Too Little Talking*: On either end of these extremes, the interviewer may not gather all the information that is really needed to make an appropriate selection decision. Structured interviews help keep this from happening. (page 228)

- *Playing District Attorney or Psychologist*: Some interviewers misuse their power by turning the interview into a game of "gotcha" or by probing for hidden meanings in everything the applicants say. Structured interviews help keep this from happening. (page 228)

7. **Explain why you think that it is (or is not) important to select candidates based on their values, as well as the usual selection criteria such as skills and experience.** The responses here may well fall into two groups: some may think it is important and other may not think it is appropriate. Those who support using values in the selection criteria should point to issues such as: each organization has values, so it is important to find candidates who support those organizational values, some values are important to the welfare of the organization (honesty, etc.). Those who do not support it will likely point to issues such as: values are a gray area and difficult to accurately measure, using values can easily lead to adverse impact against some protected groups. (pages 236-238)

Individual and Group Activities:

1. **Give a short presentation entitled "How to be Effective as an Interviewee."** There are several things you can do to get an extra edge in the interview. Preparation is essential - - learn all you can about the employer, the job, and the people doing the recruiting. Second, uncover the interviewer's real needs - - use open-ended questions. Third, relate yourself to the interviewer's needs. Fourth, think before answering. Answering should be a three step process: pause/think/speak. Fifth, appearance and enthusiasm are important. Sixth, make a good first impression, remembering the importance of non-verbal behavior.

2. **Working individually or in groups, develop a structured situational interview for hiring someone to teach a college-level course in human resource management.** The interview questions might include questions such as: "How would you handle a student who is sleeping in class?" or "What would you do if a student was disruptive in class by making inappropriate noises or talking during your lecture?" Any type of situational question that relates to classroom management or to the administrative details that a teacher must handle would be appropriate. (pages 229-230)

3. **Working individually or in groups, use the interview process described in this chapter's Small Business Applications feature to explain how you would interview a candidate for the job of President of the United States.** The process is described on pages 235-236. The answers should include developing behavioral specifications for the job, which should fall into the categories of knowledge-experience, motivation, intellectual, and personality. The questions that they design should clearly set up situations that relate to each of the behavioral specifications they developed. And there should be a clear interview plan which works through the items listed on the bottom of page 235 and the top of page 236.

Cases and Exercises:

Experiential Exercise: In-Class Mock Interview (page 240)

This exercise is well explained in step-by-step instructions in the text. It gives students the opportunity to practice developing a structured interview form and in conducting a structured interview.

Case Incident: The Out-of-Control Interview (page 241)

1. **How would you explain the nature of the panel interview Maria had to endure? Specifically, do you think it reflected a well-thought-out interviewing strategy on the part of the firm, or carelessness on the part of the firm's management? If it was carelessness, what would you do to improve the interview process at Apex Environmental?** It is fairly clear that the panel interview was a stress interview designed to see how well she could handle difficult situations. In this respect, it seems to have been a well-thought-out interviewing strategy, but there was a very clear element of carelessness on

the part of the firm's management. The panel was obviously not well-trained and was careless in the choice of questions that they used. Many of the questions were clearly discriminatory and could be used against them in a gender-based discrimination suit.

2. **Would you take the job offer if you were Maria? If you're not sure, is there any additional information that would help you make your decision, and if so, what is it?** Maria needs additional information. What she does know is the nature of the job and the clear fit with her training and skills. The additional information that she should seek involves the number of women who work at Apex, the levels of management which they have attained, and the satisfaction of those women with their treatment by the Apex management. The fact that the entire interview panel was men and their choices of questions leaves us with reservations about how she would be treated once hired.

3. **The job of applications engineer for which Maria was applying requires: (1) excellent technical skills with respect to mechanical engineering; (2) a commitment to working in the area of pollution control; (3) the ability to deal well and confidently with customers who have engineering problems; (4) a willingness to travel worldwide; and (5) a very intelligent and well-balanced personality. What questions would you ask when interviewing applicants for the job?** There are a wide variety of specific questions that could be posed to address these issues. Questions need to be job-related, specifically to the requirements listed above. They also need to clearly avoid any discriminatory areas. Questions might be speculative or job-related.

Case Application: The Lost Interview (page 241)

Two supervisors need to interview an assistant they will share. Students are asked to evaluate the interviewing style and identify areas for improvement.

1. **Is Rosa's fourth interview likely to be more successful than the first three? Why or why not?** Not likely. Rosa's first question could be very defense arousing. She needs to put the candidate at ease and get them speaking before she asks the more difficult questions?

2. **Do you see any flaws in Rosa's preparation for the interview process? In Keith's?** While the students don't have a list of Rosa's questions they can make some assumptions. For example, Keith and Rosa have some share criteria for success as well as some individual criteria. Both should have some questions that related to their evaluation criteria. It is also not uncommon to decide which person will ask a particular question. That Rosa cannot remember one of Keith's questions doesn't say much about his skill.

3. **What could Rosa and Keith do differently, both individually and as a team?** Sharing their questions and evaluation criteria ahead of time would have allowed them to consolidate their ideas and select the best question set. They also need to agree on criteria other than age. Keith appears better at getting the candidate to talk, but not at eliciting much in the way of useful material. Rosa asks meaningful questions but is unable to get the candidate to disclose themselves. A combination of their two skills would make a formidable interviewing team.

Chapter 7
Training and Developing Employees

In Brief:. This chapter is devoted to the issue of ongoing training and development of employees. Needs analysis, techniques, purposes, and evaluation are all covered. Additionally, the chapter points out the importance of new employee orientation and lists some of the important things to cover during that process.

Interesting Issues: New employee orientation has been shown to have measurable and positive effects on employee retention and satisfaction. In spite of this, many organizations do not have a formalized orientation process and each employee gets a different orientation to the organization. For those students who have been employed, it may be useful to discuss their experiences and frustrations or satisfaction with orientations.

Lecture Outline

I. **Orienting Employees**

    A. Orientation

        1. Basic Background Information

        2. Socialization

II. **The Training Process**

    A. Introduction

    B. The Five Step Training and Development Process (Figure 7.2 on page 251)

        1. Needs Analysis

        2. Instructional Design

        3. Validation

        4. Implementation

        5. Evaluation and Follow-Up

    C. Training and Learning

        1. Review of How People Learn

        2. Research Insight

    D. Legal Aspects of Training

E.   Training Needs Analysis

    1.   Task Analysis

    2.   Performance Analysis

F.   Task Analysis: Assessing the Training Needs of New Employees

    1.   Task Analysis Record Form

        a.   task list
        b.   when and how often performed
        c.   quantity, quality performance standards
        d.   conditions under which performed
        e.   skills or knowledge required
        f.   where best learned

B.   Performance Analysis: Determining the Training Needs of Current Employees

C.   The High-Performance Organization: Employee Testing and Training Program pages 256-257 of the text: see Discussion Boxes solutions at end of this chapter

IV.   Training Techniques

A.   On-the-Job Training

    1.   OJT

        a.   preparation of the learner
        b.   presentation of the operation
        c.   performance tryout
        d.   follow-up

B.   Apprenticeship Training

C.   Informal Learning

D.   Job Instruction Training

E.   Lectures

F.   Programmed Learning

G.   Audiovisual Techniques

    1.   Teletraining

    2.   Videoconference Distance Learning

     H.   Vestibule or Simulated Training

           1.   Safety

           2.   Learning Efficiency

           3.   Money

     G.   Computer-Based Training

     H.   Small Business Applications
page 262 of the text: see Discussion Boxes solutions at end of this chapter

V.   Managerial Development and Training Techniques

     A.   What is Managerial Development?

VI.   Training for Special Purposes

     A.   Literacy Training Techniques

     B.   Aids Education

     C.   Global HRM: Training for International Business
page 269 of the text: see Discussion Boxes solutions at end of this chapter

VI.   Managerial Development and Training Techniques

     A.   What is Management Development?

     B.   Managerial On-the-Job Training

           1.   Job Rotation

           2.   Coaching/Understudy Approach

           3.   Action Learning

     C.   Diversity Counts: Do Women Make Better Managers?
page 274 of the text: see Discussion Boxes solutions at end of this chapter

     D.   Managerial Off-the-Job Training and Development Techniques

           1.   The Case Study Method

           2.   Management Games

Chapter 7: Training and Developing Employees

Discussion Boxes

The High-Performance Organization: An Employee Testing and Training Program
(page 256)

This dialogue box describes one company's employee testing and training program. It is designed to train employees in those areas specifically required for their jobs, to prepare them for ISO-9000 compliance, and to foster pride and morale. Over 70 percent of the workforce has completed the training resulting in a significantly improved and effective workforce.

Small Business Applications: Training
(page 266)

This dialogue box gives a step-by-step practical procedure for small businesses to develop training programs. The five steps are: (1) Set Training Objectives; (2) Write a Detailed Job Description; (3) Develop an Abbreviated Task Analysis Record Form; (4) Develop a Job Instruction Sheet; (5) Prepare a Training Program for the Job.

Global HRM: Training for International Business
(page 266)

This dialogue box gives describes some of the prepackaged training programs for global programs. It also discusses some of the reasons for doing special global training programs.

Diversity Counts: Do Women Make Better Managers?
(page 274)

This dialogue box describes the results of research that indicates that women managers may be better transformational leaders than men. Transformational leaders "move followers to go beyond their self-interest to concerns for their group or organization."

Key Terms

employee orientation	A procedure for providing new employees with basic background information about the firm. (page 249)
training	The process of teaching new employees the basic skills they need to perform their jobs. (page 249)
task analysis	A detailed study of a job to identify the skills required so that an appropriate training program may be instituted. (page 254)
performance analysis	Careful study of performance to identify a deficiency and then correct it with new equipment, a new employee, a training program, or some other adjustment. (page 254)
on-the-job training (OJT)	Training a person to learn a job while working at it. (page 257)
job instruction training (JIT)	Listing of each job's basic tasks, along with key points in order to provide step-by-step training for employees. (page 259)
programmed learning	A systematic method for teaching job skills involving presenting questions or facts, allowing the person to respond, and giving the learner immediate feedback on the accuracy of his or her answers. (page 261)
vestibule or simulated learning	Training employees on special off-the-job equipment, as in airplane pilot training, whereby training costs and hazards can be reduced. (page 263)
management	Any attempt to improve current or future management

development	performance by imparting knowledge, changing attitudes, or increasing skills. (page 272)
succession planning	A process through which senior-level openings are planned for and eventually filled. (page 272)
job rotation	A management training technique that involves moving a trainee from department to department to broaden his or her experience and identify strong and weak points. (page 272)
action learning	A training technique by which management trainees are allowed to work full time analyzing and solving problems in other departments. (page 273)
case study method	A development method in which the manager is presented with a written description of an organizational problem to diagnose and solve. (page 275)
management game	A development technique in which teams of managers compete with one another by making computerized decisions regarding realistic but simulated companies. (page 275)
role playing	A training technique in which trainees act out the parts of people in a realistic management situation. (page 278)
behavior modeling	A training technique in which trainees are first shown good management techniques in a film, are then asked to play roles in a simulated situation, and are then given feedback and praise by their superior. (page 278)
controlled experimentation	Formal methods for testing the effectiveness of a training program, preferably with before-and-after tests and a control group. (page 281)

Discussion Questions:

1. **"A well-thought-out orientation program is especially important for employees (like recent graduates) who have had little or no work experience." Explain why you agree or disagree with this statement.** New employees can suffer from a significant amount of anxiety during the first few days on the job as they find themselves in an environment and culture that they are not acquainted with. Those with little job experience may find it especially difficult without orientation since they have little other experience on which to base their expectations. A well developed orientation program will socialize new employees into important organizational values, whereby their chances of easing smoothly into the organization are improved. (page 249)

2. **You're the supervisor of a group of employees whose task it is to assemble tuning devices that go into radios. You find that quality is not what it should be and that many of your group's tuning devices have to be brought back and reworked; your own boss says that "You'd better start doing a better job of training your workers."**
(a) What are some of the "staffing" factors that could be contributing to this problem? The problem could be related to inadequate training. Other staffing factors that could be contributing to this problem are improper selection criteria resulting in the wrong type of people being selected for the jobs. Performance criteria may be unclear or unenforced. The climate or the values may be non-productive for any number of reasons. (page 254)

(b) Explain how you would go about assessing whether it is in fact a training problem. Use performance analysis to appraise the performance of current employees while determining if training could reduce performance problems; if so, training is the place to start. Several steps are recommended in the text for accomplishing the performance analysis. In the process, you will learn whether it is a "can't do" or "won't do" situation. Other factors in the motivation model would also need to be assessed, including the working conditions and quality of supervision. (page 257)

3. **Explain how you would apply our principles of learning in developing a lecture, say, on orientation and training.** Student answers should reflect the issues identified in the guidelines on page 260. As an exercise, you might have students develop and deliver a lecture (perhaps on one section of this chapter). Then ask the students to critique each other based on the guidelines summarized on page 260.

4. **John Santos is an undergraduate business student majoring in accounting. He has just failed the first accounting course, Accounting 101, and is understandably upset. Explain how you would use performance analysis to identify what, if any, are John's training needs.** The first thing that needs to be determined is if this is a "can't do" or a "won't do" situation. It is possible that as a first-year student, John has spent more time socializing and not enough time studying. This would indicate a need for training on studying skills and prioritization. It is also possible that John really does not have the necessary basic skills that he needs in order to be successful in this course. This could be determined through some testing to see if he has the prerequisite knowledge and skills. If it is a problem, remedial training or courses would be appropriate. A third possibility is that John simply does not really have the interest or natural inclinations that would make him successful in the accounting area. This could be determined through some testing and career interest surveys. If this is the case, training is not appropriate, but rather John should be counseled to change majors. (page 254)

5. **What are some typical on-the-job training techniques? What do you think are some of the main drawbacks of relying on informal on-the-job training for breaking new employees into their jobs?** The most common is the understudy or coaching technique. Others include apprenticeship training and job rotation. There are several possible drawbacks to OJT: (1) not every employee will get the same basic information, in fact, some may not get basic, fundamental information; (2) the quality of the training is highly dependent on the training skills of the employee who supervises the OJT...and that person's skills and training are usually not in the area of training; (3) the new employee may get false information or detrimental inculturation depending on the employees that they conduct their OJT with. (page 257)

6. **This chapter points out that one reason for implementing special global training programs is the need to avoid lost business ". . . due to cultural insensitivity." What sort of cultural insensitivity do you think is referred to and how might that translate into lost business?** The cultural insensitivities would include cross-cultural values, assumptions concerning communication, identity issues, etiquette, lifestyles, style of dress, etc. Any of these can result in unintentional insults or offending people which can easily make those people reluctant to do business with you. (page 269)

    What sort of training program would you recommend to avoid such cultural insensitivity? There are a wide variety of programs and consultants that specialize in these areas. It is important to have someone who is knowledgeable in these areas conduct the training to assure that the correct information and guidance is given. (page 269)

7. **This chapter presents several examples of how diversity training can backfire, such as "the possibility of post-training participant discomfort." How serious do you think potential negative outcomes like these are and what would you do as an HR manager to avoid them?** If the training is not properly conceived and conducted, these negative outcomes can be very serious. They can lead to resignations of members of under-represented groups, lawsuits, and poor morale and productivity. It is important that these outcomes be avoided by utilizing experts in diversity for developing the training program, and only using people who have been thoroughly trained and are culturally aware and sensitive to conduct the training.

8. **How does the involvement approach to attitude surveys differ from simply administering surveys and returning the results to top management?** Please note: This question should not be used as the text does not address this issue.

9. **Compare and contrast three organizational development techniques.** Please note: This question should be in Chapter 8, but due to an editing error, ended up in this chapter. Chapter 8 identifies OD techniques as: sensitivity training, team building, confrontation meetings, survey research, technostructural interventions, action research, and strategic interventions.

10. **Describe the pros and cons of five management development methods.** Job rotation: broadens experience and helps the candidate find what he or she prefers. Coaching/Understudy: works directly with the person he or she will replace, helps assure trained managers are ready to assume key positions. Action Learning: allows special projects to be handled. Case Study Method: classroom oriented, gives real-life situations, allows analysis and reflection. Management Games: learn by getting involved, competition, emphasizes the need for planning, problem-solving skills, teamwork. Outside Seminars: CEUs, developed by experts, time away from pressures of work. University-Related Programs: certifications and degrees, theoretical knowledge, sharing with students from other industries. Role Playing: opportunity to work through probable situations, negative views of role-playing. Behavior Modeling: effective, learning and skill development, reinforces decisions immediately. In-House Development Centers: tailored to the needs of the company, expensive. Students should be able to come up with additional pros and cons for each method.

11. **Discuss the key alternatives in a typical off-the-job management development program.** Basically, companies or employees will have choices of case-study, management games, outside seminars, university-related programs, role playing, or behavior modeling. Choosing which one will be dependent on the types of skills or knowledge needed. Accounting may be best learned in a university-related program, while interpersonal skills might be better learned through role playing.

12. **Do you think job rotation is a good method to use for developing management trainees? Why or why not?** Most students will probably support job rotation for management trainees. It gives the trainee the opportunity to experience several areas and to develop cross-departmental skills and cooperation. It also give the trainee the chance to experience different areas to see what he or she likes.

Individual and Group Activities:

1. **Pick out some task with which you are familiar – moving the lawn, tuning a car – and develop a job instruction training sheet for it.** There is an example of a job instruction training sheet for operating a large motorized paper cutter on pages 257 and 258 of the text. Students should be able to put the task they select into the format given.

2. **You are to give a short lecture on the subject "Guidelines to Keep in Mind When Presenting a Lecture." Give a five or ten-minute lecture on the subject making sure, of course, to follow the guidelines as enumerated in this chapter.** Students should integrate the points listed on page 258 into their lecture. It would be useful to have classmates evaluate each other using these guidelines.

3. **Working individually or in groups, you are to develop a short programmed learning program on the subject "Guidelines for Giving a More Effective Lecture." Use the example in Figure 7-4 and any other information you may have available to develop your programmed learning program.** Students should use the guidelines listed on page 260, but should not forget that this assignment is not just listing guidelines. They are to develop a programmed learning that 1) presents questions, facts, or problems to the learner, 2) allows the person to respond, and 3) provides feedback to the learner on the accuracy of his or her answers.

4. **Working individually or in groups, contact a provider of management development seminars such as the American Management Association. Obtain copies of their recent listings of seminar offerings. At what levels of managers do they aim their seminar offerings? What seems to be the most popular types of development programs? Why do you think that's the case?** Depending on the provider contacted, the results of this exercise will vary. It would be a good idea to assign different groups or individuals to different providers to assure that you get a variety of responses. It may be useful to have a class discussion about the differences that they found.

5. **Working individually or in groups, develop a series of concrete examples to illustrate how a professor teaching human resource management could use at least eight of the management development techniques described in this chapter in teaching his or**

her HR course. Student results will again vary. Look for examples to be well thought out and to represent the guidelines given on page 260 of the text.

6. **Check with several local community colleges to determine what if any apprenticeship programs they are partners in.** Help students to understand that skilled labor programs are technical, involve significant skills, often require high levels of math, and are vital to economic development.

Cases and Exercises

Experiential Exercise: Developing a Training Program (page 284)

This exercise will give students the opportunity to experience the activities involved in creating a training program. As with any exercise, students may rush through and brush aside details, or they might painstakingly address all the details needed. Look for quality and for those that take the time to deal with the details that make a program a success.

Case Incident: Reinventing the Wheel at Apex Door Company (page 285)

1. **What do you think of Apex's training process? Could it help to explain why employees "do things their way" and if so, how?** There is a weak accountability system. The person assigned to perform training is likely to very low motivation (a departing employee). With no formal descriptions the trainer will teach "their way" of accomplishing tasks. There is no training documentation. One receives training in "how to train." There are no outcomes measures to determine if the training was successful.

2. **What role do job descriptions play in training?** Job descriptions set the boundaries of jobs in terms of required knowledge and skills. By understanding the job description, a trainer can define the learning requirements for a new or transitioning employees.

3. **Explain in detail what you would do to improve the training process at Apex (make sure to provide specific suggestions, please).** Every position would have a formal (written) description. Training procedures would be documented for each position. Supervisors would be formally accountable for training.

Case Application: A Training and Development Problem at Sumerson Manufacturing
(page 286)

Sumerson Manufacturing is planning on opening a new plant in 16 months. You have been asked to develop a plan to recruit, select and train the approximately one thousand new workers that will be needed over the next three years.

1. **Develop a plan outline of how to hire and train an entire staff of new employees below the second level of management in one year and have them ready to open the new**

plant? Students will need to draw from several chapters. In order to develop a hiring plan, the company will need to have identified specific jobs and the knowledge and skills associated with those jobs. Some students will likely recommend that Sumerson review their existing jobs. Bright students will note that Sumerson will move some of its best employees to the new plant (this raises an interesting set of issues about what the culture will be like in the existing plants).

The training plan will likely involve the 5 steps noted in the chapter:
1. Needs analysis
2. Instructional design
3. Validation
4. Implementation
5. Evaluation & follow-up

2. **How should you go about procuring the balance of the thousand employees needed to staff the plant by the projected full-operations date?** HR will want to involve the supervisors at the new plant and get their input in any recruiting plan. The plant provides an opportunity for Sumerson to review its prior practices and establish new benchmarks.

Chapter 8
Managing Organizational Renewal

In Brief: This chapter discusses the issues of organizational change and development. TQM, team-based organizations, process reengineering, and flexible work arrangements are discussed.

Interesting Issues: Sensitivity training and other organizational development techniques often create unintended controversy. Companies seek to change attitudes, values, and beliefs, in order to improve performance, customer services or other areas. However, it care is not exercised, those attempts to change attitudes, values, and beliefs can be viewed as an intrusion and forcing "political correctness" on employees who may hold fundamental beliefs in areas such as homosexuality, abortion, sexuality, etc.

Lecture Outline

I. **Managing Organizational Change and Development**

    A.   What to Change? HR's Role

          1.   Strategic Change

          2.   Cultural Change

          3.   Structural Change

          4.   Task Redesign

          5.   Technological Change

          6.   Changes in People, Attitudes, and Skills

    B.   A 10-Step Process for Leading Organizational Change

          1.   Kurt Lewin's 3-Step Process

               a.   Unfreezing
               b.   Moving
               c.   Refreezing

          2.   10-Step Process

               a.   Establish a Sense of Urgency
               b.   Mobilize Commitement to Change through Joint Diagnosis
               c.   Create a Guiding Coalition
               d.   Develop a Shared Vision

    e. Communicate the Vision

    f. Enable Employees to Facilitate the Change

    g. Generate Short-Term Wins

    h. Consolidate Gains and Produce More Change

    i. Anchor the New Ways of Doing Things in the Company's Culture

    j. Monitor Progress and Adjust the Vision as Required

  C. Using Organizational Development to Change Organizations

    1. What it Organizational Development?

    2. Human Process Applications

    3. Sensitivity Training

    4. Team Building

    5. Technostructural Interventions

    6. Human Resource Management Applications

    7. Strategic Applications

II. Instituting Total Quality Management Programs

  A. Total Quality Management Programs

    1. Total Quality Management

    2. Implementing TQM at Florida Power and Light

  B. Human Resource Management and the Quality Improvement Effort

    1. Lessons from FPL

    2. HR's Role in Winning the Baldrige Award

    3. HR and ISO 9000

III. Creating Team-Based Organizations

  A. The Nature of Self-Directed Teams and Worker Empowerment

  B. The High-Performance Organization: HR
    pages 304-305 of the text: see Discussion Boxes solutions at end of this chapter

  C. Global HRM: Extending Participative Decision Making Abroad
    pages 306-307 of the text: see Discussion Boxes solutions at end of this chapter

Discussion Boxes:

The High-Performance Organization: HR
(page 304)

This box describes the Product Improvement Teams at Kaiser Electronics. Lessons learned by product improvement teams have led to improved company design guides and handbooks and to improved maintenance schedules and procedures.

Global HRM: Extending Participative Decision Making Abroad
(pages 306-307)

Techniques that may work in one country may actually backfire in another. It is important to recognize the different values and attitudes that the different cultures bring to the table about management and decision making.

Key Terms

strategic change	A change in a company's strategy, mission and vision. (page 292)
cultural change	A change in a company's shared values and aims. (page 292)
structural change	The reorganizing-redesigning of an organization's departmentalization, coordination, span of control, reporting relationships, or centralization of decision making. (page 293)
technological change	Modifications to the work methods an organization uses to accomplish its tasks. (page 293)
organizational development interventions	HR-based techniques aimed at changing employees' attitudes, values, and behavior. (page 293)
organizational development (OD)	A method aimed at changing attitudes, values, and beliefs of employees so that employees can improve the organizations. (page 296)
sensitivity training	A method for increasing employees' insights inro their own behavior by candid discussions in groups led by special trainers. (page 297)
team building	Improving the effectiveness of teams such as corporate officers and division directors through use of consultants, interviews, and team-building meetings. (page 298)
confrontation meetings	A method for clarifying and bringing into the open iner-group misconceptions and problems so that they can be resolved. (page 298)
survey research	A method that involves surveying employees' attitudes and providing feedback to the work groups as a basis for problem analysis and action planning. (page 298)

total quality management (TQM)	A type of program aimed at maximizing customer satisfaction through continuous improvements. (page 300)
Malcolm Baldridge Award	An award created by the U.S. Department of Commerce to recognize quality efforts of U.S. companies. (page 300)
functional team	A quality improvement team composed of volunteers who typically work together as natural work units. (page 301)
cross-functional team	A quality improvement team formed to address problems that cut across organizational boundaries. (page 301)
lead team	A quality improvement team headed by a vice president or other manager that serves as a steering committee for all the teams that operate in its area. (page 301)
self-directed team	A work team that uses consensus decision making to choose its own team members, solve job-related problems, design its own jobs, and schedule its own break time. (page 304)
business process reengineering (BPR)	The redesign of business processes to achieve improvements in such measures of performance as cost, quality, service, and speed. (page 309)
flextime	A plan whereby employees build their workday around a core of midday hours. (page 311)
four-day workweek	An arrangement that allows employees to work four ten-hour days instead of the more usual five eight-hour days. (page 312)
job sharing	A concept that allows two ot more people to share a single full-time job. (page 312)
telecommuting	A work arrangement in which employees work at remote locations, usually at home, using video displays, computers, and other telecommunications equipment to carry out their responsibilities. (page 312)
flexyears	A work arrangement under which employees can choose (at six month intervals) the number of hours they want to work each month over the next year. (page 313)

Discussion Questions:

1. There are several ways a company can initiate change, some of which are strategic change, cultural change, structural change, and technological change. Define three types of change and explain how they can help and organization change for the

better. Each of the three is described on pages 292-293 with a definition and a discussion of how they can help a firm.

2. **What steps would you take to institute self-directed work teams?** The steps outlined in the "High-Performance Organization" discussion box are a good guide. Kaiser Electronics conducts a 7-day team-building event to launch a new team and develop its mission and vision. Their teams sponsor and leader are trained in problem-solving, job design, interviewing skills, and reading financial reports. Teams meet frequently, normally five times per week.

3. **Explain the pros and cons of flextime and the four-day workweek.** There are a full three paragraphs on page 311 describing the pros and cons of flextime. Page 312 also has three paragraphs devoted to the pros and cons of the four-day workweek.

Individual and Group Activities:

1. **Working individually or in groups, develop an organizational change program for improving service in an area of your university or college that you feel is in need of improvement.** Students should clearly identify and define the problem and clearly indicate which type of change they are going to implement: strategic, cultural, structural, or technological. They need to demonstrate a good understanding of the change method used.

2. **Define "reengineering." Working individually or in groups, develop a brief example of how you would reengineer a familiar process such as class enrollment at the start of the semester.** "The fundamental rethinking and radical redesign of business processes to achieve dramatic improvements in critical, contemporary measures of performance such as cost, quality, service, and speed." Look for creativity and solid analysis in their examples. (page 309)

Cases and Exercises

Experiential Exercise: Unfreezing an Ogranization (pages 314-315)

Students should enjoy and perform well in this exercise. For each stakeholder, students should identify reasons related to their job, union, tenure, pay, or status that they might resist change. For example, the sales force would probably resist change because it might threaten their salaried pay status. There might be a real fear that you will move to commissions. Long-term employees might fear change because they have only known one way to do things and are not sure if they could perform differently. Look for students to analyze and look at things from each stakeholder's point of view.

Case Incident: "We're Getting Nowhere Fast" (page 315)

1. **Which organizational change and development techniques discussed in chapter 8 would you recommend Mr. Star use to try to determine what the problems are at the**

company? Please be specific. Star needs to diagnose the organization and determine if the issues require an intervention at the strategic level, cultural level or group/interpersonal level. He might use techniques like action research, employee feedback surveys, interviews and process reviews.

2. **Given the admittedly limited information in the incident, would you recommend that Star implement a team-based organization? Why or why not?** A team based organization could work, but it would require major changes in the philosophy, control systems and culture of the company. There are several other actions Star could take to improve performance including changes in the way performance is appraised and rewarded.

3. **Do you think it would be helpful for Star to implement a total quality management program? Be prepared to tell Mr. Star what the pros and cons of implementing such a program in his company might be?** Quality has increasingly become a necessary (but not sufficient) requirement for success. Star's company cannot afford to overlook quality, so in one sense, quality management is not an option. Advantages of a quality management system include: better trained employees, greater employee involvement and commitment, improved quality of products and services. The disadvantages are: TQM is not a substitute for good management – Star still needs to have an appropriate strategy and structure; the process is very time consuming and requires executive involvement; there is no guarantee of improvements in efficiency or early improvements in productivity; and the company needs to make a substantial commitment to education.

Case Application: Is the Honeymoon Over at Flat Rock? (page 316)

Mazda had opened a plant in Flat Rock, Michigan, a suburb of Detroit in the early 1980s. The plant had great promise and was expected to employ thousands of employees. But by 1990, conditions had seriously deteriorated. The operation was on its fourth labor relations director and union was boycotting the suggestion box (a hallmark of Japanese management).

1. **What do you think accounts for the fact that with all the plant's emphasis on teamwork and on total quality the personnel problems were still so serious?** There appear to be a number of potential reasons. There is generally a lack of dialog between the Americans and Japanese and between the workers and managers. This has resulted in a breakdown of trust. The Union may have exploited this lack of trust, helping workers interpret Japanese productivity as a means of reducing jobs. There are also substantial cultural differences between the Japanese style of management and the US style. US managers interpreted the lack of autonomy as a rejection of their ideas.

2. **As the consultant to the new Ford plant manager, outline a detailed plan (based in large part on the contents of this chapter) for transforming the culture and Flat Rock and for making the plant more productive?** The text outlines a ten step process for leading organizational change that will work as a framework for this case illustration.
   1. Establish a sense of urgency
   2. Mobilize commitment by jointly diagnosing the business
   3. Create a guiding coalition
   4. Develop a shared vision

5. Communicate the vision
6. Enable employees to facilitate the change
7. Generate short term wins
8. Consolidate gains and produce more change
9. Anchor new ways of doing things in the company's culture
10. Monitor progress and adjust the vision as required.

Some students may also wish to invoke the Lewin model in regard to the issue of unfreezing the existing culture.

Chapter 9
Appraising Performance

In Brief: This chapter gives a good coverage of the performance appraisal process and the different tools and methods available.

Interesting Issues: Despite lots of attention, money and effort, performance appraisals remain an area with which few managers or employees are satisfied. This may be worth discussing. Is it just that we don't have a good enough system yet, is there an intrinsic problem with performance appraisals, or is it just human nature to dislike them?

Lecture Outline

I.   The Appraisal Process

    A.   The Supervisor's Role in Appraisal

    B.   Steps in Appraising Performance

        1.   Define the Job

        2.   Appraise Performance

        3.   Provide Feedback

        4.   Performance Appraisal Problems

            a.   Didn't Define the Job
            b.   Didn't Appraise Performance
            c.   Didn't Provide Feedback

        5.   How to Clarify What Performance You Expect

II.   Appraisal Methods

    A.   Graphic Rating Scale Method

    B.   Alternation Ranking Method

    C.   Paired Comparison Method

    D.   Forced Distribution Method

    E.   Critical Incident Method

    F.   Narrative Forms

    G.   Behaviorally Anchored Rating Scales (BARS)

1. Five Steps to Develop

    a. generate critical incidents
    b. develop performance dimensions
    c. reallocate incidents
    d. scale the incidents
    e. develop final instrument

2. Advantages

    a. more accurate gauge
    b. clearer standards
    c. feedback
    d. independent dimensions
    e. consistency

H. The Management by Objectives (MBO) Method

1. Six Main Steps

    a. set the organization's goals
    b. set departmental goals
    c. discuss departmental goals
    d. define expected results
    e. performance reviews
    f. provide feedback

2. Problems To Avoid

    a. setting unclear, unmeasurable objectives
    b. time consuming
    c. tug of war

I. Mixing the Methods

J. Information Technology and HR: Computerized Performance Appraisals and Electronic Performance Monitoring. pages 336-337 of the text: see Discussion Boxes solutions at end of this chapter

III. Appraising Performance: Problems and Solutions

A. Dealing with the Rating Scale Appraisal Problems

1. Unclear Standards

2. Halo Effect

3. Central Tendency

4. Leniency or Strictness

5. Bias

6. Research Insight: Pregnancy and Performance Appraisals

7. Table 9-3 on page 341 gives important similarities and differences, advantages and disadvantages of different appraisal tools.

B. How to Avoid Appraisal Problems

1. Become Familiar with the Problems

2. Choose the Right Appraisal Tool

3. Train Supervisors

4. Diary Keeping

C. Legal and Ethical Issues in Performance Appraisal

D. Who Should Do the Appraising?

1. Appraisal b the Immediate Supervisor

2. Using Peer Appraisals

3. Rating Committees

4. Self-Ratings

5. Appraisal by Subordinates

6. Research Insight: Effectiveness of Upward Feedback

7. 360-degree Feedback

8. The High-Performance Organization: The 360-Degree Performance Management System. page 346 of the text: see Discussion Boxes solutions at end of this chapter

IV. The Appraisal Interview

A. Types of Interviews

1. Satisfactory—Promotable

        2.   Satisfactory—Not Promotable

        3.   Unsatisfactory—Correctable

    B.   How to Prepare for the Appraisal Interview

        1.   Assemble the Data

        2.   Prepare the Employee

        3.   Choose the Time and Place

    C.   How to Conduct the Interview

        1.   Be Direct and Specific

        2.   Don't Get Personal

        3.   Encourage the Person to Talk

        4.   Don't Tiptoe Around

    D.   How to Handle a Defensive Subordinate

    E.   How to Criticize a Subordinate

    F.   How to Ensure That the Appraisal Interview Leads to Improved Performance

    G.   How to Handle a Formal Written Warning

V.   Performance Appraisal in Practice

VI.   The Role of Appraisals in Managing Performance

    A.   Do Appraisals Really Help to Improve Performance?

    B.   TQM-Based Appraisals for Managing Performance

Discussion Boxes:

Information Technology and HR: Computerized Performance Appraisals and Electronic Performance Monitoring
(pages 336-337)

This box describes new software programs that help the supervisor create the performance appraisal. The programs allow the supervisor to record critical incidents throughout the year, and then use them again as they develop the appraisal.

The High-Performance Organization: The 360-Degree Performance Management System
(page 346)

This box describes the implementation of a 360-degree performance appraisal systems that was implemented by Rock Island Arsenal. How the program was developed as well as how it works is outlined.

Key Terms

graphic rating scale	A scale that lists a number of traits and a range of performance for each. The employee is then rated by identifying the score that best describes his or her performance for each trait. (page 323)
alternation ranking method	Ranking employees from best to worst on a particular trait. (page 325)
paired comparison method	Ranking employees by making a chart of all possible pairs of the employees for each trait and indicating which is the better employee of the pair. (page 327)
forced distribution method	Similar to grading on a curve; predetermined percentages of ratees are placed in various categories. (page 327)
critical incident method	Keeping a record of uncommonly good or undesirable examples of an employee's work-related behavior and reviewing it with the employee at predetermined times. (page 329)
behaviorally anchored rating scale (BARS)	An appraisal method that aims at combining the benefits of narrative and quantified ratings by anchoring a quantified scale with specific narrative examples of good and poor performance. (page 331)
management by objectives (MBO)	Involves setting specific measurable goals with each employee and then periodically reviewing the progress made. (page 333)
unclear performance standards	An appraisal scale that is too open to interpretation; instead, include descriptive phrases that define each trait and what is meant by standards like "good" or "unsatisfactory." (page 337)

halo effect	In performance appraisal, the problem that occurs when a supervisor's rating of a subordinate on one trait biases the rating of that person on other traits. (page 338)
central tendency	A tendency to rate all employees the same way, avoiding the high and the low ratings. (page 338)
strictness / leniency bias	The problem that occurs when a supervisor has a tendency to rate all subordinates either high or low. (page 338)
bias	The tendency to allow individual differences such as age, race, and sex to affect the appraisal rates these employees receive. (page 339)
appraisal interviews	An interview in which the supervisor and subordinate review the appraisal and make plans to remedy deficiencies and reinforce strengths. (page 347)

Discussion Questions:

1. **Discuss the pros and cons of at least four performance appraisal tools.** The text lists eight different performance appraisal tools. Students might discuss the pros and cons of any four of these eight. The tools are described on pages 323 - 334. (An example of some of the pros and cons is: Graphic Rating Scale method is easy to use, simple, and does not take much time to administer. However, different supervisors may interpret a numerical rating differently and the traits rated may or may not relate to performance.)

2. **Explain how you would use the alternation ranking method, the paired comparison method, and the forced distribution method.** The alternation method would be used by listing all employees to be rated, deciding who is the best in a trait to be rated, and which is the worst. Then decide who is the second best, and the second worst ... the third best and the third worst ... and so on until all the employees have been ranked for that trait. Then do the same with the next trait to be rated. With the paired comparison, for each trait to be rated, the supervisor would have a sheet with employee names in pairs ... every employee name is paired with every other name. For each pair, the supervisor would circle the one of the two that is better in that trait. Forced Distribution gives the supervisor a set rating scale (such as 1 through 5). The supervisor is limited to giving a pre-determined percentage of his or her employees' rating. For example: 15% can get a 1, 20% can get a 2, 30 % can get a 3 ... and so forth. (pages 325-238)

3. **Explain in your own words how you would go about developing a behaviorally anchored rating scale.** Each student should express the five steps in his or her own words. Those five steps are: 1) generate critical incidents; 2) develop performance dimensions; 3) reallocate incidents; 4) scale the incidents; and 5) develop final instrument. (pages 331-333)

4. **Explain the problems to be avoided in appraising performance.** The five main rating scale problems listed in the text are: 1) unclear standards; 2) halo effect; 3) central tendency; 4) leniency or strictness; and 5) bias. (pages 337-339)

5. **Discuss the pros and cons of using different potential raters to appraise a person's performance.** The advantages of using several raters (either a rating committee, or a combination of peer, supervisor, and subordinate ratings) is that the ratings tend to be more valid than those of one individual rater. The negatives might include the time and cost involved as well as problems with the amount of daily contact that some raters may not have with the employee being rated.

6. **Explain the four types of appraisal interview objectives and how they affect the way you manage the interview.** Note: There are only **three** types outlined in the text! Each interview objective is tied to the type of appraisal being given. When the performance is satisfactory and the employee is promotable, the objective is to make development plans. This is the easiest interview to manage. You will discuss the person's career plans and develop a specific action plan for the educational and professional development the person needs to move to the next job. When the performance is satisfactory but the employee is not promotable, the objective is to maintain performance. This can be a more difficult interview to manage. You will need to find incentives that are important to the individual to help maintain the satisfactory performance. When the person's performance is unsatisfactory but correctable, the objective is to lay out an action plan for correcting the performance. This involves identifying the performance or behaviors that are problematic, informing the employee of the expected behavior or performance, and developing a plan for implementing the new performance or behaviors. (pages 346-347)

7. **Explain how to conduct an appraisal interview.** There are four things listed in the text to keep in mind: 1) be direct and specific; 2) don't get personal; 3) encourage the person to talk; 4) don't tiptoe around. Students should expound on these basic principles of conducting the interview. These are followed with four "how to" items that are important as well...how to: handle a defensive subordinate, criticize a subordinate, ensure that the appraisal interview leads to improved performance, handle a formal written warning. (pages 347-349)

8. **Answer the question: "How would you get the interviewee to talk during an appraisal interview?** There are several techniques that will help: 1) stop and listen to what the person is saying ... don't be afraid of a little silence; 2) ask open-ended questions; 3) use prompting statements like "go on," or "tell me more;" 4) restate the person's last statement as a question. (page 348)

Group and Individual Activities:

---

1. **Working individually or in groups, develop a graphic rating scale for the following jobs: secretary, engineer, directory assistance operator.** Job characteristics may include, but not be limited to: *Secretary*--quantity of work, frequency of errors, attendance, and initiative; *Engineer*--initiative, significance of contribution to the organization, problem

solving skills, frequency of errors, and communication skills; *Directory Assistance Operator*- -speed, attendance, accuracy, and friendliness. In each case, the students should come up with a defining statement that clarifies what the job characteristic means. (pages 323 & 324)

2. **Working individually or in groups, evaluate the rating scale in Table 9-2. Discuss ways to improve it.** There are many things that might be suggested for improvements. These suggestions might include, but not be limited to: clearer explanation of the rating scale, provide behavioral anchors for the scale points, and rework the items so that several questions about specific behaviors for each item. (page 342)

3. **Working individually or in groups, develop, over the period of a week, a set of critical incidents covering the classroom performance of one of your instructors.** If you had the class conduct a job analysis and create a job description for an instructor in Chapter 3, it would be helpful to refer to that to help identify what kinds of behavior and tasks the instructor should be doing. This will give a good basis for students to observe and watch for critical incidents. If they find critical incidents that are not based in these other documents, it will be a good opportunity to go back and review how all this ties together and that we haven't communicated to the instructor in the job description these behaviors or tasks that they are now wanting to rate them for.

Cases and Exercises

Experiential Exercise: Performance Appraisal (page 355)

Students are asked to review a performance appraisal form and to develop an appraisal form.

1. In evaluating the appraisal form in Figure 9-10, there are several issues that students might note for possible improvements: consider reducing the rating scale from seven points to four or five points, be more specific about subjects to be rated (e.g.: How do you rate the interest of the teacher in the subject?), and use behavioral anchors to clearly define what behaviors or actions you are rating.

2. Students should develop their own tool for appraising the performance of an instructor. Look for them to apply concepts discussed in this chapter.

3. Students should present their tools to the class. How similar are the tools? Do they all measure about the same factors? Which factor appears most often? Which do you think is the most effective tool? Encourage students to reflect on the factors that they chose, or did not choose. Share your perspective on what makes good teaching.

Case Incident: Back with a Vengeance (page 356)

1. **Could a company with an effective appraisal process have missed so many signals of instability over several years? Why or why not?** For an appraisal process to capture these signals, it would have had to measure some aspect of the employee's interpersonal

relationships, anger, outbursts, etc. Many appraisal systems focus exclusively on job related outcomes. In this case, if an employee were producing standard or higher outcomes, his interpersonal problems might not be noted.

2. **What safeguards would you build into your appraisal process to avoid missing such potentially tragic signs of instability and danger?** Personnel systems need to record any anti-social behaviors that inhibit an employee or his or her colleagues from effectively doing their jobs. In addition to the problem of workplace violence (which is of course the most serious issue) there should also be concern on the part of management to not allow a hostile work environment to develop.

3. **What would you do if confronted during an appraisal interview by someone who began making threats regarding his or her use of firearms?** I would excuse myself. Tell the person I want to finish this conversation and that I would be right back. (I would not want to call security in front of the person as it might further anger them). I would get to the nearest telephone, call security, and explain the situation. I would have security make sure of my safety before I resumed my conversation. I would want the employee to receive professional counseling to assure that the company or the supervisor was not facing the threat of retribution for their actions.

Case Application: Appraising the Secretaries at Sweetwater U (page 357)

1. **Do you think that the experts' recommendations will be sufficient to get most of the administrators to fill out the rating forms properly? Why or Why not? What additional actions (if any) do you think will be necessary?** While controversial, the recommendations would, in fact, encourage administrators to fill the forms out correctly. Using the more detailed form and not tying the performance ratings to salary increases would allow the managers to feel more free about rating the secretaries accurately. There would, however, need to be some strong training sessions (both for administrators and secretaries) to help them understand the new system. Since all secretaries have traditionally received the same salary increases, and have been pleased with that, it would be advisable to consider lowering the maximum increase to an amount that could be given to all secretaries while staying within budget. Then all secretaries with a satisfactory rating or better would receive that increase.

2. **Do you think that Vice President Winchester would be better off dropping graphic rating forms, substituting instead one of the other techniques we discussed in this chapter such as a ranking method?** Certainly other methods could be used. He has already had a taste of what would result if he went to a forced distribution or other ranking method. A BARS system might be best, but it could be costly to develop if the clerical staff have positions that are significantly different.

3. **What performance appraisal system would you develop for the secretaries if you were Rob Winchester? Defend your answer.** If the development costs are not too great, the BARS system would give the strongest solution to the current situation. The behavioral anchors would make it more difficult to just rate everyone at the top. It would also help to eliminate the different interpretations of what the rating scales mean.

Chapter 10
Managing Careers and Fair Treatment

In Brief: This chapter gives good advice and tools for managing careers. It also covers the issue of building communications with employees through guaranteed fair treatment programs and employee discipline. Proper handling of dismissals and separations, including retirement are explored.

Interesting Issues: While today many employees are retiring earlier, many experts believe that the next generation will have to retire later in order to continue to fund the retirement of those retiring now. Social Security has already increased the ages at which future generations will be eligible for benefits.

Lecture Outline

I. **The Basics of Career Management**

Table 10-1 on page 363 summarizes how activities such as training and appraisal can be used to provide career planning and development.

    A.   Roles in Career Development.
        Table 10-2 on page 364 outlines the various roles in career development.

        1.   Individual

        2.   Manager

        3.   Employer/Organization

    B.   Avoid Reality Shock.

    C.   Provide Challenging Initial Jobs.

    D.   Provide Realistic Job Previews in Recruiting.

    E.   Be Demanding.

    F.   Provide Periodic Job Rotation and Job Pathing.

    G.   Do Career-Oriented Performance Appraisals.

    H.   Provide Career Planning Workshops and Career Planning Workbooks.

    I.   Provide Mentoring Opportunities.

II. **Managing Promotions and Transfers**

    A.   Making Promotion Decisions

        1.   Decision 1: Is Seniority or Competence the Rule?

        2.   Decision 2: How is Competence Measured?

        3.   Decision 3: Is the Process Formal or Informal?

        4.   Decision 4: Vertical, Horizontal, or Other?

  B.   Diversity Counts: In Promotion and Career Management
       pages 368-369 of the text: see Discussion Boxes solutions at end of this chapter

  B.   Handling Transfers

        1.   Reasons for Transfers

        2.   Effects on Family Life

  C.   Career Management and Commitment

        1.   Developmental Activities

        2.   Career-Oriented Appraisals

        3.   Career Records/Jobs Posting System

III.   **Managing Fair Treatment**

  A.   Introduction: The Building Blocks of Fairness

  B.   Build Two-Way Communications

        1.   "Speak-Up!" Programs

        2.   What's Your Opinion?

        3.   Top-Down Programs

  C.   The High-Performance Organization: Communications
       page 374 of the text: see Discussion Boxes solutions at end of this chapter

  D.   Emphasize Fairness in Disciplining

        1.   Discipline
             Figure 10-4 on page 377 contains Discipline Guidelines.

        2.   Discipline Without Punishment

  E.   Manage Employee Privacy

Human Resource Management

IV. Managing Dismissals

    A.   Grounds for Dismissal

        1.   Unsatisfactory Performance

        2.   Misconduct

        3.   Lack of Qualifications

        4.   Changed Requirements of the Job

        5.   Insubordination

    B.   Avoiding Wrongful Discharge Suits
        guidelines on pages 380-382

    C.   The Termination Interview

        1.   Guidelines for the Termination Interview

                a.   plan the interview carefully
                b.   get to the point
                c.   describe the situation
                d.   listen
                e.   review all elements of the severance package
                f.   identify the next step

        2.   Outplacement Counseling

        3.   Exit Interviews

    D.   Layoffs and the Plant Closing Law

        1.   The Plant Closing Law

        2.   Bumping/Layoff Procedures

        3.   Alternatives to Layoffs

    E.   Adjusting to Downsizings and Mergers

        1.   Downsizing

        2.   Handling the Merger/Acquisition

    F.   Retirement

Discussion Boxes:

Diversity Counts: In Promotion and Career Management
(pages 368-369)

This discussion box explores the "glass ceiling" with respect to the promotional opportunities granted to women. It outlines in good detail possible causes as well as action plans to remedy the problem. It is recommended that all students read and understand the issues presented here. Possible discussion questions include: "Have you seen this type of discrimination?" and "What can you do to succeed anyway?"

The High-Performance Organization: Communications
(page 375)

Companies such as The Crystal Gateway Marriott Hotel are communicating financial information to employees. The associates feel involved and informed and has increased the ability to manage financial issues as the associates now have a shared undertstanding and purpose.

Key Terms

career planning and development	The deliberate process through which a person becomes aware of personal career-related attributes and the lifelong series of stages that contribute to his or her career fulfillment. (page 363)
reality shock	Results of a period that may occur at the initial career entry when the new employee's high job expectations confront the reality of a boring, unchallenging job. (page 364)
speak up! programs	Communications programs that allow employees to register questions, concerns, and complaints about work-related matters. (page 374)
opinion surveys	Communication devices that use questionnaires to regularly ask employees their opinions about the company, management, and work life. (page 374)
top-down programs	Communications activities including in-house television centers, frequent roundtable discussions, and in-house newsletters that provide continuing opportunities for the firm to let all employees be updated on important matter regarding the firm. (page 375)

discipline	A procedure that corrects or punishes a subordinate because a rule of procedure has been violated. (page 375)
dismissal	Involuntary termination of an employee's employment with the firm. (page 378)
termination at will	The idea, based in law, that the employment relationship can be terminated at will by either the employer or the employee for any reason. (page 378)
insubordination	Willful disregard or disobedience of the boss's authority or legitimate orders; criticizing the boss in public. (page 379)
wrongful discharge	An employee dismissal that does not comply with the law or does not comply with the contractual arrangement stated or implied by the firm via its employment application forms, employee manuals, or other promises. (page 380)
termination interview	The interview in which an employee is informed of the fact that he or she has been dismissed. (page 382)
outplacement counseling	A systematic process by which a terminated person is trained and counseled in the techniques of self-appraisal and securing a new position. (page 383)
plant closing law	The Worker Adjustment and Retraining Notification Act, which requires notifying employees in the event an employer decides to close its facility. (page 384)
layoff	A situation in which there is a temporary shortage of work and employees are told there is no work for them but that management intends to recall them when work is again available. (page 384)
bumping/layoff	Detailed procedures that determine who will be laid off if no work is available; generally allows employees to use their seniority to remain on the job. (page 384)
voluntary reduction in pay plan	An alternative to layoffs in which all employees agree to reductions in pay to keep everyone working. (page 385)
voluntary time off	An alternative to layoffs in which some employees agree to take time off to reduce the employer's payroll and avoid the need for a layoff. (page 385)
rings of defense	An alternative layoff plan in which temporary supplemental employees are hired with the understanding that they may be laid off at any time. (page 385)

downsizing	Refers to the process of reducing, usually dramatically, the number of people employed by the firm. (page 385)
retirement	The point at which a person gives up one's work, usually between the ages of 60 to 65, but increasingly earlier today due to firms' early retirement incentive plans. (page 386)
preretirement counseling	Counseling provided to employees who are about to retire, which covers matters such as benefits advice, second careers, and so on. (page 386)

Discussion Questions:

1. **Explain career-related factors to keep in mind when making the employee's first assignments.** 1) Avoid Reality Shock; 2) Provide Challenging Initial Jobs; 3) Provide Realistic Job Previews in Recruiting; 4) Be Demanding; 5) Provide Periodic Job Rotation and Job Pathing; 6) Do Career-Oriented Performance Appraisals; 7) Provide Career Planning Workshops and Career Planning Workbooks; 8) Provide Opportunities for Mentoring. (pages 364-366)

2. **Describe specific techniques you would use to foster top-down communication in an organization.** While this chapter talks a lot about two-way communication techniques, remember that this question is not about two-way communication, it is about top-down communication. Techniques that can be used to convey the top-down communication include: newsletters and plant-wide information meetings. The most important thing is that the organization learns to trust its employees and to give them more information. (page 375)

3. **Describe the similarities and differences between discipline without punishment and a typical discipline procedure.** The similarities are many: both have rules and policies that are established regarding employee conduct and performance, both have progressive steps to work through in cases of problems. The discipline without punishment method attempts to avoid "punishing," and encourage gaining the employee's acceptance of the rules and reminding them of the need for their compliance.

4. **Explain how you would ensure fairness in disciplining, discussing particularly the prerequisites to disciplining, disciplining guidelines, and the new "discipline without punishment" approach.** A fair discipline process is based on three prerequisites: rules and regulations, a system of progressive penalties, and an appeals process. Inform employees ahead of time as to what is and is not acceptable behavior. Progressive penalties range from oral warnings to written warnings to suspension from the job to discharge; the severity is a function of the severity of the offense and, in some cases, the number of times the offense has occurred. Discipline guidelines include the need to determine whether there was "just cause" for disciplinary action by: 1) using discipline in line with the way management usually response to similar incidents; 2) warning the employee of the consequences of the alleged misconduct; 3) punishing for violation of rules that are "reasonably related" to the efficient and safe operation of the work environment; 4) investigating adequately; 5) applying rules and employee's past history. Fairness is built into the system of discipline without punishment, in that the punitive nature of discipline is

reduced, while there is an attempt to gain the employee's acceptance of the rules. (pages 375-377)

Individual and Group Activities:

1. **Develop a resume for yourself, using the guidelines presented in this chapter. (See the Appendix)** Refer students to guidelines that are in Appendix B (pages 662-665). Look for resumes that not only meet these suggestions, but that are also error-free, attractive, and spotlight the students' achievements.

2. **Write a one-page essay stating, "Where I would like to be career-wise 10 years from today."** Help students to be realistic. There is a fine line between motivational high goals and realistic understanding of the work world. However, it trying to bring reality, keep humble and remember that Fred Smith, founder of Federal Express, developed the proposal for his company in a college course and received a "C." The instructor told him that the project was supposed to be something that was realistic. (page 364)

3. **Working individually or in groups, choose three occupations (such as management consultant, HR manager, or salesperson) and use some of the sources described in this chapter to make an assessment of the future demand for this occupation over the next ten years or so. Does this seem like a good occupation to pursue? Why or why not?** Students should be able to support their conclusions with data and information from these sources.

4. **Working individually or in groups, choose several occupations such as programmer, lawyer, or accountant and identify as many job openings for these occupations on the Internet as you can. Do you think the Internet is a valuable job search source for these occupations? Why or why not?** The question that you are likely to have to deal with is whether those that don't find anything didn't because there was little or no information on the net relating to their assigned occupation, or because they did not do a good job of searching. Because of this, it is recommended that you conduct a search yourself for the same occupations to be able to evaluate this aspect of their work.

5. **Working individually or in groups, obtain copies of the student handbook for this college and determine to what extent there is a formal process through which students can air grievances. Do you think the process should be an effective one? Based on your contacts with other students, has it been an effective grievance process?** Again, depending on the organization, the answers will be different. Check student answers for understanding of the principle elements of fair treatment programs. (pages 374-378)

6. **Working individually or in groups, determine the nature of the academic discipline process in this college. Do you think it is an effective one? Based on what you read in Chapter 16, would you recommend any modification of the student discipline process?** Student answers should reflect an understanding of the principle of fairness in disciplining (page 375), discipline guidelines (page 377), discipline without punishment (page 376), and managing dismissals (pages 378-382).

Cases and Exercises

Experiential Exercise: Disciplinary Actions (pages 388-389)

This exercise describes a situation where an employee made a critical error for which she was suspended for three days and a previously approved promotion was revoked. The arbitrator upheld the suspension, but reinstated the promotion. Of primary importance here is the issue of past practice. Point out to students that for both actions, the primary issue for the arbitrator was not "what should have been done," but "what has been done in the past." This is why it is critical to be consistent and to clearly communicate any changes in policy in advance.

Case Incident: Job Insecurity at IBM (page 389)

1. **What do you think accounts for the fact that a company like IBM can have high job security but still lose market share, sales and profitability? In other words, why do you think job security did not translate into corporate success as well as it might have at IBM?** There are a number of important issues here. First, there is little in the literature to suggest that job security is sufficient to keep employees at peak performance. Second, the issue of job security, while important, does not take into account the dynamics of the market. While a company may have exemplary HR practices, it still must pay close attention to the actions of its competitors, suppliers, host governments, etc.

2. **What steps do you think IBM could have taken in order to continue to avoid layoffs? If you don't think any such steps were feasible, explain why?** IBM appeared to respond very slowly to changes in the environment. Had IBM envisioned, for example, the change toward PCs, they may have reduced their hiring in the 1970s of mainframe computer workers. This would have made IBM less overstaffed. Some students will argue that these steps are not feasible. Few businesses have perfect foresight into market changes. No business can legally attain perfect insight into the proposed actions of their competitors. As such, business will need to react to changes in the markets. Opponents of this view will argue that the expenses created by a downturn in the market should be borne by the risk holders (shareholders) and not employees.

3. **Given IBM's experience with its full employment policy, what do you think are the implications for other companies thinking of instituting full employment policies of their own?** It is a very difficult policy to imagine maintaining. Companies will likely consider the failure of IBM as a sufficient reason not to pursue such a policy. However, in a tight labor market, an enterprising company may offer lifetime employment as a means of differentiating itself in the labor market and therefore enable it to attract superior human resources.

Case Application: The Mentor Relationship Turns Upside Down (page 390)

1. **Is there any evidence in the case that Carol's assumptions about Walter's feelings regarding the situation are correct?** Carol knew she would have to undue many of Walter's decisions. There is no specific evidence in the case of how Walter might respond to this, but Carol has had a long-term professional relationship with him and will likely have seen him in similar situations.

2. **What advice would you offer Carol for approaching Walter?** Carol will likely feel a debt of gratitude to Walter for his help. She will likely want to maintain a positive working relationship with Walter. She might be able to help Walter process some of his feelings and frustrations by asking him about difficulties they might encounter in their working relationship? She may wish to ask a general question like, "How do you think you will respond if I feel I need to undo some of your original decisions. Carol has shown skill in the past at helping subordinates get over the initial awkwardness of the situation by meeting one on one.

3. **What should Carol's ultimate goal be in this assignment?** Regardless of her not wanting to hurt Walter's feelings, she is still charged with the success of the venture.

4. **Assume Carol has heard a rumor that Walter has considered resigning. What (if anything) should she do about it?** Though Walter was not successful in this venture, his position suggests he has had many other successes in the firm. Most companies would not want to lose someone with Walter's experience and expertise. She may wish to consult with her supervisors and inform them what she has heard and discuss strategies for retaining Walter. If her personal relationship with him is strong, she may wish to confront him with the rumor directly, probe his reasons for leaving and try to identify what it would take to keep Walter and his expertise with company.

Chapter 11
Establishing Pay Plans

In Brief: This chapter covers the basics of compensation. Included are basic considerations in determining pay rates, establishing pay rates, current trends in compensation, pricing managerial and professional jobs, and current issues in compensation management.

Interesting Issues: This chapter lists and discusses many current and controversial issues in compensation management. You may want to incorporate a discussion of the current issues described on pages 421-423.

Lecture Outline

I.   Basic Aspects of Compensation

      A.   Compensation at Work

II.   Basic Factors in Determining Pay Rates

      A.   Legal Considerations in Compensation

            1.   1931 Davis-Bacon Act

            2.   1936 Walsh-Healey Public Contract Act

            3.   1938 Fair Labor Standards Act

                  a.   overtime pay
                  b.   minimum wage
                  c.   maximum hours
                  d.   equal pay
                  e.   record-keeping
                  f.   child-labor

            4.   1963 Equal Pay Act

            5.   1964 Civil rights Act

            6.   1974 Employee Retirement Income Security Act (ERISA)

            7.   The Tax Reform Act of 1986

            8.   Other Legislation Affecting Compensation

      B.   Union Influence on Compensation Decisions

      C.   Compensation Policies

    D.   Equity and Its Impact on Pay Rates

          1.   Five Step Process:

                a.   salary survey
                b.   job evaluation
                c.   pay grades
                d.   wage curves
                e.   fine tune pay rates

III.   Establishing Pay Rates

    A.   Step 1. Conduct the Salary Survey

          1.   Introduction

          2.   Commercial, Professional, and Government Salary Surveys
                Table 11-1 on page 402 shows a sample compensation survey.

          3.   Using the Internet to Do Compensation Surveys

    B.   Step 2. Determine the Worth of Each Job: Job Evaluation

          1.   Purpose of Job Evaluation

          2.   Compensable Factors

          3.   Planning and Preparation for the Job Evaluation

          4.   Ranking Method of Job Evaluation
                Table 11-1 on page 406 gives a sample of job ranking.

                a.   pros and cons

          5.   Job Classification (or Grading) Evaluation Method
                Figure 11-2 on page 407 shows a sample grade definition.

          6.   Point Method of Job Evaluation

          7.   Factor Comparison Job Evaluation Method

          8.   Computerized Job Evaluations

    C.   Step 3. Group Similar Jobs into Pay Grades

    D.   Step 4. Price Each Pay Grade—Wage Curves
                Figure 11-3 on page 409 shows a sample wage curve

    E.   Step 5. Fine Tune Pay Rates

        1.   Developing Rate Ranges
                Table 11-2 on page 410 shows a sample pay schedule.
                Figure 11-4 on page 410 shows a sample wage structure.

        2.   Correcting Out-of-Line Rates

IV.   Current Trends in Compensation

    A.   Skill-Based Pay

        1.   Competence Testing

        2.   Effect of Job Change

        3.   Seniority and Other Factors

        4.   Advancement Opportunities

    B.   Broadbanding
           Figure 11-5 on page 414 shows a sample of setting three bands.
           Figure 11-6 on page 414 shows a sample of assigning values to jobs in bands.
           Figure 11-7 on page 414 shows a sample of positioning pay within a band.

    C.   Information Technology and HR
           page 415 of the text: see Discussion Boxes solutions at end of this chapter

    D.   Why Job Evaluation Plans Are Still Widely Used

    E.   The High-Performance Organization: Compensation Management
           Pages 416-417 of the text: see Discussion Boxes solutions at end of this chapter

    F.   A Glimpse into the Future—The "New" Pay

V.   Pricing Managerial and Professional Jobs

    A.   Compensating Managers

        1.   Basic Compensation Elements
              a.   salary
              b.   benefits
              c.   short-term incentives
              d.   long-term incentives
              e.   perquisites

        2.   Managerial Job Evaluation

    B.   Compensating Professional Employees

VI.   **Current Issues in Compensation Management**

     A.   The Issue of Comparable Worth

         1.   The Issue

         2.   The Gunther Supreme Court Case

         3.   Comparable Worth and Job Evaluation

         4.   Implications

     B.   The Issue of Pay Secrecy

     C.   The Issue of Cost-of-Living Differentials

     D.   Global Issues in HR: The Issue of Compensating Expatriate Employees
            Page 424 of the text: see Discussion Boxes solutions at end of this chapter

     E.   Small Business Applications: Developing a Pay Plan
            Pages 425-427 of the text: see Discussion Boxes solutions at end of this chapter

         1.   Developing a Workable Pay Plan

         2.   Compensation Policies

         3.   Legal Issues

Discussion Boxes:

Information Technology and HR: Websites for Compensation Management
(page 415)

This discussion box gives a list of websites devoted to compensation-related matters. You may want to assign students to look up the sites and report on what is available there, or possibly have them find additional sites as well.

The High-Performance Organization: Compensation Management
(pages 416-417)

This box describes how IBM used compensation management as part of the plan to renew the organization. IBM had dominated the industry in the 1970s and early 1980s but lost touch with the customers by the late 1980s. Changing the pay structure played a major role in changing the organization to meet the new needs of the late 1990s.

Global HRM: The Issue of Compensating Expatriate Employees
(page 424)

Managers who are placed in other countries face a wide variance of costs of living. The issue of cost-of-living differentials becomes exaggerated with the even larger differences of costs of living between countries. This box describes two basic policies that are popular for dealing with these issues: home-based and host-based policies.

Small Business Applications: Developing a Pay Plan
(pages 425-427)

This box discusses some of the basic approaches that a small business can use to implement the concepts discussed in this chapter. It includes practical direction on developing a workable pay plan, compensation policies, and a discussion of legal issues.

Key Terms

---

employee compensation	All forms of pay or rewards going to employees and arising from their employment. (page 396)
Davis-Bacon Act	A law passed in 1931 that sets wage rates for laborers employed by contractors working for the federal government. (page 396)
Walsh-Healey Public Contract Act	A law enacted in 1936 that requires minimum-wage and working conditions for employees working on any government contract amounting to more than $10,000. (page 397)
Fair Labor Standards Act	Congress passed this act in 1936 to provide for minimum wages, maximum hours, overtime pay, and child labor protection. The law has been amended many times and covers most employees. (page 397)
Equal Pay Act of 1963	An amendment to the Fair Labor Standards Act designed to require equal pay for women doing the same work as men. (page 422)
Civil Rights Act	This law makes it illegal to discriminate in employment because of race, color, religion, sex, or national origin. (page 398)
Employee Retirement Income Security Act (ERISA)	The law that provides government protection of pensions for all employees with company pension plans. It also regulates vesting rights (employees who leave before retirement may claim compensation from the pension plan). (page 398)

salary survey	A survey aimed at determining prevailing wage rates. A good salary survey provides specific wage rates for specific jobs. Formal written questionnaire surveys are the most comprehensive, but telephone surveys and newspaper ads are also sources of information. (page 400)
benchmark job	A job that is used to anchor the employer's pay scale and around which other jobs are arranged in order of relative worth.(page 400)
job evaluation	A systematic comparison done in order to determine the worth of one job relative to another. (page 403)
compensable factor	A fundamental, compensable element of a job, such as skills, effort, responsibility, and working conditions. (page 404)
ranking method	The simplest method of job evaluation that involves ranking each job relative to all other jobs, usually based on overall difficulty. (page 405)
classification (or grading) method	A method for categorizing jobs into groups. (page 406)
classes	Dividing jobs into classes based on a set of rules for each class, such as amount of independent judgment, skill, physical effort, and so forth, required for each class of jobs. Classes usually contain similar jobs--such as all secretaries. (page 406)
grades	A job classification system synonymous with class, although grades often contain dissimilar jobs, such as secretaries, mechanics, and firefighters. Grade descriptions are written based on compensable factors listed in classification systems, such as the federal classification system. (page 406)
grade definition	Written descriptions of the level of, say, responsibility and knowledge required by jobs in each grade. Similar jobs can then be combined into grades or classes. (page 406)
point method	The job evaluation method in which a number of compensable factors are identified and then the degree to which each of these factors is present on the job is determined. (page 407)
factor comparison method	A widely used method of ranking jobs according to a variety of skill and difficulty factors, then adding up these rankings to arrive at an overall numerical rating for each given job. (page 407)
pay grade	A pay grade is comprised of jobs of approximately equal difficulty. (page 408)

wage curve	Shows the relationship between the value of the job and the average wage paid for this job. (page 409)
rate ranges	A series of steps or levels within a pay grade, usually based upon years of service. (page 409)
comparable worth	The concept by which women who are usually paid less than men can claim that men in comparable rather than strictly equal jobs are paid more. (page 421)

Discussion Questions:

1. **What is the difference between exempt and non-exempt jobs?** Under the Fair Labor Standards Act, certain categories of employees are exempt from the act or certain provisions of the act. Those categories of employees that are exempted from provisions of the act are called "exempt" while those covered by the act are called "non-exempt." Generally executives, administrative, managerial, and professional employees are exempt from minimum wage and overtime provisions. (page 397)

2. **Should the job evaluation depend on an appraisal of the jobholder's performance? Why or Why not?** No. Job evaluation involves comparing jobs to one another based on their content. Individual performance is covered under performance evaluation and does not affect the content of the job. (pages 403-404)

3. **What is the relationship between compensable factors and job specifications?** Compensable factors include skill, effort, responsibility, working conditions, problem solving, know-how, accountability, and the like. Many of these factors are obtainable from job specifications which are part of the job analysis. (pages 404)

4. **What are the pros and cons of the following methods of job evaluation: ranking, classification, factor comparison, point method?** The ranking method is the simplest, easiest to explain, and the quickest to implement. The drawbacks to the ranking method are a tendency to rely to heavily on guestimates and it does not provide a yardstick for measuring the relative values of jobs. The classification (or grading) method is simple, and widely used. Most employers usually end up classifying jobs anyway, so this method often makes sense. The disadvantages are that it is difficult to write the class or grade descriptions and considerable judgment is required to apply them. The factor comparison method is considered a refinement of the ranking system, thus it may be considered to be more accurate than others. The disadvantages are the considerable time and effort involved to implement the system and to evaluate jobs. The point method, like the factor comparison method, is a quantitative analysis that is considered accurate. This system is easy to implement, but developing a point manual can be an expensive (pages 405-408)

5. **In what respect is the factor comparison method similar to the ranking method? How do they differ?** In the factor comparison method, the evaluators rank each job several times, once for each compensable factor. They differ, in that the factor comparison method is a quantitative technique which involves multiple rankings for each job. The ranking

method usually uses only one compensable factor and simply involves making a judgment on the ranking of one job relative to others in the firm on that job's worth to the organization. Ranking is the easiest method, although it provides no yardstick for the comparison of one job relative to another. (pages 405-408)

6. **What are the pros and cons of broadbanding, and would you recommend your current employer (or some other firm you're familiar with) use it? Why or why not?** The advantages are that is injects greater flexibility into employee compensation and it is especially sensible where firms have flattened their organizations. It allows training and rotation of employees with fewer compensation problems. It also facilitates the bondaryless jobs and organizations being embraced by many firms. The negatives are that it may be more difficult to administer and keep track of individuals and to keep pay comparable. (pages 413-415)

7. **It was recently reported in the news that the average pay for most university presidents ranged around $200,000 per year, but that a few earned closer to $500,000 per year. What would account for such a disparity in the pay of universities' chief executive officers?** The same things that account for the wide range of pay for the chief executive officers of other businesses and organizations in the same industry. Many factors enter into this mix, including, but not limited to: size of the organization, ownership of the organization (public or private), focus of the organization (religious or secular, research or teaching), performance of the organization (financial and enrollment), prestige of the organization, and endowment and funding of the organization.

Group and Individual Activities:

1. **Working individually or in groups, conduct salary surveys for the following positions: entry-level accountant and entry-level chemical engineer. What sources did you use, and what conclusions did you reach? If you were the HR manager for a local engineering firm, what would you recommend that you pay for each job?** Students should be expected to use several of the resources indicated on pages 400-401 for gathering this information. Results should be checked for bias or contamination such as only surveying the largest firms in the area, or the unwillingness of some firms to provide this information. Student recommendations should be based on sound logic and conclusion from the data they collect. (pages 400-401)

2. **Working individually or in groups, use the BLS area wage surveys to determine local area earnings for the following position: File Clerk I, Accounting Clerk II, Secretary V. How do the BLS figures compare with comparable jobs listed in your Sunday newspaper? What do you think accounts for any discrepancy?** You should check the BLS listings yourself to assure that students get the correct numbers. Any discrepancies might be explained by: cost of living differentials within the BLS area, company size and competitiveness, actual grade of the position advertised may not coincide with BLS grades, economic changes within the year since publication, and other factors.

8. **Working individually or in groups, use the ranking method to evaluate the relative worth of the jobs listed in Question 7, above. (You may use the Dictionary of Occupational Titles as an aid.) To what extent do the local area earnings for these jobs correspond to your evaluations of the jobs?** While there may be discrepancies, most rankings would probably be (from lowest to highest): File Clerk I, Secretary V, Accounting Clerk II, although there could be an argument to switch the last two.

Cases and Exercises:

Experiential Exercise: Job Evaluations (page 429)

This exercise will give students experience in performing a job evaluation using the ranking method. When students have completed this exercise in their small groups, you should consider comparing results and discussing the similarities and differences.

Case Incident: Salary Inequities at Acme Manufacturing (page 430)

1. **What would you do if you were Blankenship?** This should generate lively discussion. Few students will argue for a "do nothing" approach, as the risk of legal damages is too high. Some students will argue that the discrepancies in salaries will not remain secret. If this is true, then women supervisors will discover they are underpaid and may seek additional back pay. Some students will suggest the company inform the supervisors that as a result of a recent compensation study, it was determined that these jobs were underpaid. The women in question will receive a larger raise at the time of their next performance review. Students in favor of this proposal will argue that by making it public but deferring the adjustment, they will signal that it is not a major crisis.

2. **How do you think the company got into a situation like this in the first place?** The informal system suggests that the local culture has overly influenced the compensation process. Issues like whether a spouse is working are not part of a professional compensation practice.

3. **Why would you suggest Blankenship pursue the alternative you suggested?** Students will provide a variety of reasons. Those suggesting back pay as well as a raise will argue that:
   a. The company needs to maintain fairness (a social justice approach).
   b. They will signal to employees that unfair practices will not be tolerated.
   c. They will gain the support of a group of stakeholders.
   Those suggesting raises but no back pay may argue:
   a. The women will likely feel their needs have been addressed.
   b. It will be less expensive.
   c. It will be less likely to draw a negative response from White males.
   d. If the women push for back wages, they can be granted later.

Case Application: Salary Administration in the Engineering Department (page 431)

Majestic is a multi-location chemical company. The more than one hundred engineers in the engineering department perform services for many of Majestic's locations. The case reviews Majestic's compensation package for engineers. Tom Green is concerned that if he rewards new employees based on potential, he will not have sufficient funds for his senior employees.

1. **What do you think of Majestic's Salary Administration Policy? How would you change it?** There are many obvious benefits to Majestic's program. It is well organized, well documented, promotes fairness across divisions, strives for internal as well as external equity and has elements that facilitate management control. It is weak in that the criteria used for new employee evaluation are subjective. With a "pool" system, experienced engineers end up competing for dollars, matching their performance against the potential of new employees.

2. **Would you recommend broadbanding for engineer jobs at Majestic? Why or why not?** There will be some disagreement over this as the case has limited information about the other plants. Students opposed to broadbanding will argue that it would need to be applied across all plants to maintain internal equity. Those opposed would argue the merits of broadbanding, including its usefulness as a compensation system when working with self-directed work teams from differing levels in the organization (a normal occurrence for an engineering group).

3. **How would you proceed now if you were Tom Green?** There will likely be lively discussion of this decision. Some will suggest that in the short term, Tom needs to make sure that he has more input into the salary distribution system. The salary administrator does not have to live with the immediate consequences the salary distribution decision. In the longer term, Tom needs to work with Majestic to develop a system that will allow him to reward high potential employees (based on a more objective criteria) while still being able to reward those who have made career contributions.

Chapter 12
Pay-for-Performance and Financial Incentives

In Brief: This chapter gives an overview of money and motivation, then outlines different incentive programs that are used for different types of employees. It also discusses organization-wide incentive plans.

Interesting Issues: There is tension between the concept of providing employees with a secure, stable income (which some feel allows them the ability to be entrepreneurial and take appropriate risks for the company), and the idea of linking pay directly to performance. A good discussion may be developed from this tension as students grapple with their own resolution of this issue.

Lecture Outline

I. **Money and Motivation: Background**

    A. Performance and Pay

    B. Types of Incentive Plans

        1. Individual Incentive Programs

        2. Spot Bonuses

        3. Group Incentive Programs

        4. Profit-Sharing Plans

        5. Gainsharing Programs

        6. Variable pay

II. **Incentives for Operations Employees**

    A. Piecework Plans

        1. Straight Piecework Plan

        2. Guaranteed Piecework Plan

        3. Advantages and Disadvantages

    B. Standard Hour Plan

    C. Team or Group Variable Pay Incentive Plans

III. Incentives for Managers and Executives

A.   Short-Term Incentives: The Annual Bonus

1.   How Much to Pay Out (Fund Size)

2.   Deciding Individual Awards

B.   Long-Term Incentives

1.   Capital Accumulation Programs

2.   Stock Options
Figure 12-1 on page 447 shows business purposes of stock option plans.

3.   Other Plans

4.   Performance Plans

5.   Long-Term Incentives: Cash vs. Stock Options

6.   Long-Term Incentives for Overseas Executives

7.   Relating Strategy to Executive Compensation

IV. Incentives for Salespeople

A.   Salary Plan

B.   Commission Plan

1.   Research Insight

C.   Combination Plan

V. Incentives for Other Professionals and Employees

A.   Merit Pay As An Incentive

1.   Merit Pay: Two New Options

a.   One lump sum payment per year.
Table 12-1 on page 454 shows an award determination matrix.
b.   Tie awards to both individual and organizational performance.

2.   Usually based on individual performance

B.   Incentives for Professional Employees

VI.   Organization Wide Variable Pay Plans

A.   Profit-Sharing Plans

B.   Employee Stock Ownership Plan (ESOP)

C.   The High Performance Organization: Sharing the Wealth
Pages 456-457 of text. See discussion boxes solution at the end of this chapter.

D.   Scanlon Plan

1.   Philosophy of Cooperation

2.   Identity

3.   Competence

4.   Involvement System

5.   Sharing of Benefits Formula

E.   Gainsharing Plans

1.   Steps in Gainsharing Plan

a.   Establish General Plan Objectives
b.   Define Specific Performance Measures
c.   Formulating the Funding Formula
d.   Determine Method for Dividing and Distributing
e.   Make Size of Payment Meaningful
f.   Choose Form of Payment
g.   Decide on Frequency of Payment
h.   Develop the Support or Involvement System

2.   Making the Plan Work

F.   At-Risk Variable Pay Plans

VII.   Developing More Effective Incentive Plans

A.   When to Use Incentives

1.   When Effort and Output Are Clearly Related

2.   When The Job Is Standardized, Work Flow Is Regular, Delays Are Rare

3.   Quality Is Less Important Than Quantity, Or Quality Can Be Measured

B.   Why Incentive Plans Don't Work

    1.   Reasons
        a.   Performance Pay Can't Replace Good Management
        b.   You Get What You Pay For
        c.   Pay Is Not A Motivator
        d.   Rewards Punish
        e.   Rewards Rupture Relationships
        f.   Rewards Can Unduly Restrict Performance
        g.   Rewards May Undermine Responsiveness
        h.   Rewards Undermine Interest and Motivation
        i.   People Work For More Than Money

    2.   Commitment and Incentives

    3.   Small Business Applications: Adapt Incentives to the FLSA
Pages 463-464 of the text. See discussion boxes solutions at the end of chapter

    4.   Consider the Company's Situation

    5.   Stress Productivity and Quality Measures if Possible

    6.   Get Employee Input In System Design

C.   Incentive Plans In Practice

D.   The High-Performance Organization: Incentive Plans
       Pages 465-466 of the text: See discussion boxes solutions at the end of chapter

Discussion Boxes

The High-Performance Organization: Sharing the Wealth
(pages 456-457)

Thermacore has been successful in recent years and management is convinced that at least part of the success is due to an employee bonus program and a stock ownership program. This box gives some details of both program, but the interesting thing is that the bonus program gives the same dollar bonus to all employees, regardless of income, seniority, or position in the company.

Small Business Applications: Adapt Incentives For Non-Exempts to the FLSA
(pages 463-464)

This box outlines problems that the FLSA has created for companies that use incentive pay as a part of their employee regular pay. A major issue is that those incentive payments usually must be counted as part of the base pay when computing overtime pay. The discussion box gives an example to clarify this confusing issue.

The High-Performance Organization: Incentive Plans
(pages 465-466)

This box outlines Federal Express' compensation plan. It lists seven different pay-for-performance programs that Fed Ex has as part of its plan. All programs, with the exception of the merit program, are paid in one-time, lump-sum awards.

Key Terms

---

fair day's work	Frederick Taylor's observation that haphazard setting of piecework requirements and wages by supervisors was not sufficient, and that careful study was needed to define acceptable production quotas for each job. (page 439)
scientific management	The careful, scientific study of the job for the purpose of boosting productivity and job satisfaction. (page 439)
spot bonus	A spontaneous incentive awarded to individuals for accomplishments not readily measured by a standard. (page 440)
variable pay	Any plan that ties pay to productivity or profitability, usually as one-time lump payments. (page 440)
piecework	A system of pay based on the number of items processed by each individual worker in a unit of time, such as items per hour or items per day. (page 441)
straight piecework plan	Under this pay system each worker receives a set payment for each piece produced or processed in a factory or shop.(page 441)
guaranteed piecework plan	The minimum hourly wage plus an incentive for each piece produced above a set number of pieces per hour. (page 441)
standard hour plan	A plan by which a worker is paid a basic hourly rate, but is paid an extra percentage of his or her base rate for production exceeding the standard per hour or per day. Similar to piecework payment, but based on a percent premium. (page 442)
team or group incentive plan	A plan in which a production standard is set for a specific work group, and its members are paid incentives if the group exceed the production standard. (page 442)

annual bonus	Plans that are designed to motivate short-term performance of managers and are tied to company profitability. (page 443)
capital accumulation	Long-term incentives most often reserved for senior executives.
programs	Six popular plans include stock options, stock appreciation rights, performance achievement plans, restricted stock plans, phantom stock plans, and book value plans. (page 443)
stock option	The right to purchase a stated number of shares of a company stock at today's price at some time in the future. (page 443)
merit pay (merit raise)	Any salary increase awarded to an employee based on his or her individual performance. (page 452)
profit-sharing plan	A plan whereby most employees share in the company's profits. (page 454)
employee stock ownership plan (ESOP)	A corporation contributes shares of its own stock to a trust in which additional contributions are made annually. The trust distributes the stock to employees on retirement or separation from service. (page 455)
Scanlon plan	An incentive plan developed in 1937 by Joseph Scanlon and designed to encourage cooperation, involvement, and sharing of benefits. (page 457)
gainsharing plan	An incentive plan that engages employees in a common effort to achieve productivity objectives and share the gains. (page 458)

Discussion Questions:

1. **Compare and contrast six types of incentive plans.** Various types of incentive plans were presented in the text, including piecework plans, straight and guaranteed plans, standard hour plans, plans for salespersons (commissions and combination plans), and group incentive plans. With the piecework plans, earnings are tied directly to what the individual worker produces, and are more appropriate in a manufacturing organization. Commissions are more appropriate for salespeople in situations where they are largely unsupervised. In group incentive plans like the Scanlon Plan, all workers involved in developing and implementing cost savings share in the benefits of the suggestions. (pages 440-460)

2. **Explain five reasons why incentive plans fail.** When incentive plans fail, it can be for a variety of reasons like: employees do not believe that effort will obtain the reward, bad management overrides the plan, rewards tied to the wrong measures, plan is complicated

and difficult for employees to understand, or standards are too high or too low. See the list on page 462 for more reasons and details. (pages 461-463)

3. **Describe the nature of some important management incentives**. Two widely used management incentive plans are merit pay and profit sharing plans. Merit pay is any salary increase that is awarded to an employee on his or her individual performance. Advocates argue that only pay tied directly to performance can motivate improved performance. Profit sharing plans distribute a portion of the company's profits to employees in the form of a bonus. Research shows that benefits are more subtle than increased productivity—possibly in the form of better worker commitment. There are additional management incentive plans students might cover, including long-term incentives such as capital accumulation plans, various alternative stock plans, and performance plans. (pages 443-449)

4. **When and why would you pay a salesperson a salary and commission combined?** Salary plans work well when your objective is prospecting work or where the salesperson is primarily involved in account servicing. They are often found in industries that sell technical products. A commission plan is appropriate when sales costs are proportional to sales. This can reduce the selling investment for fixed costs. The straight commission also provides salespeople with the greatest possible incentive and there is a tendency to attract high-performing people. Combination plans are used when the firm wants to direct its salespeople's activities by detailing what services the salary component is being paid for while the commission component provides a built-in incentive. (pages 451-452)

5. **What is merit pay? Do you think it's a good idea to award employees merit raises? Why or why not?** Merit pay is a salary increase that is awarded to an employee based on his or her individual performance. It is a good idea to award merit raises when you have a good performance appraisal system and employees' individual effort can be fairly and accurately evaluated or measured. (pages 452-454)

6. **In this chapter we listed a number of reasons experts give for not instituting a pay-for-performance plan (such as "rewards punish"). Do you think these points (or any of them) are valid? Why or why not?** All of these reasons are, or can be, valid. There will also be organizational situations where one or more of them will not be valid. Students should describe situations in which the reason is (or is not) valid. (page 462)

7. **What is a Scanlon plan? Based on what you've read in this book so far, what features of a commitment-building program does the Scanlon plan include?** This is an incentive plan that was developed in 1937 by Joseph Scanlon. It includes features such as a philosophy of cooperation, identity, competence, involvement, and sharing of benefits. All these are features of a commitment-building program. The Scanlon plan is actually an early version of what today is known as a gainsharing plan. (pages 457-458)

8. **Suppose your instructor decided to award final grades to teams of students in this class, instead of to individuals. What would be the pros and cons of such an approach? Would you like the idea?** This is a good question for students to be able to step out of the idealism they sometimes have about concepts and into the reality that the concepts create. This approach would encourage students to work together (which is an important skill they need to have as they go into the working world), and to learn from each

other. The negatives include the dependence on the quality of their teammates and the lack of individual accountability.

Individual and Group Activities:

1. **Working individually or in groups, develop an incentive plan for the following positions: chemical engineer, plant manager, used-car salesperson. What factors did you have to consider in reaching your conclusions?** I would give the chemical engineer a merit raise system because he or she has little perceived control or impact over the production or profitability of the company. The plant manager should receive an annual bonus tied to the profitability of the plant, as well as a stock option plan to encourage long-term planning as well. The used-car salesperson would likely receive a straight commission plan because sales are more directly dependent on his or her ability to sell those cars to prospective customers.

2. **A state university system in the southeast recently instituted a "Teacher Incentive Program" (TIP) for its faculty. Basically, faculty committees within each university college were told to award $5,000 raises (not bonuses) to about 40% of their faculty members based on how good a job they did teaching undergraduates and how many they taught per year. What are the potential advantages and pitfalls of such an incentive program? How well do you think it was accepted by the faculty? Do you think it had the desired effect?** This program would put a premium on undergraduate teaching as opposed to research or graduate teaching. If it were to work, the best teachers would be motivated to teach at the undergraduate level in order to increase their earnings. The pitfalls are many. Some research or graduate faculty may actually make more through consulting or other outside means, thus they will not be motivated by this system. If research is important to this organization, or the graduate programs are vital, this program could damage those programs. The awarding of the moneys is likely to be inconsistent because specific guidelines have not been spelled out. More likely, the rewarding of the raises may become more political as the committees who have other values determine the awards. It is very likely that the system was met with great opposition by the faculty.

Cases and Exercises:

Experiential Exercise: Analyze a Compensation System
(pages 468-469)

This exercise presents a fictional auto dealership and problems that they are experiencing with customer satisfaction and quality. Students are to analyze the current compensation system to see if it contributes to the problem.

1. **In what ways might your group's compensation plan contribute to the customer services problems?** *Sales force*: pay is based almost entirely on commission. The salesperson has no motivation to assist customers who they do not believe will result in a sale. *Finance office*: bonuses for getting customers to use the company financing encourage

finance people to coerce people into making that choice. *Detailing*: pay is based entirely on the number of cars detailed per day. There is no measure of quality, nor requirement of it regarding pay. *Mechanics*: pay is based almost entirely on number of cars serviced as well as servicing them faster than the standard estimated repair time. There is no measurement of quality or accuracy of repairs. *Receptionist/phone service people*: straight hourly rate does not have any performance rewards.

2. **Are there rewards that your department provides that impede the work of other departments?** In every case, there is no link between incentives and quality of work performed. This results in poor quality which affects the other departments.

3. **What recommendations would you make to improve the compensation system in a way that would likely improve customer satisfaction?** The dealership already has a customer satisfaction survey in place. They need to link results from quality measures to the incentives that their employees receive. Examples are: *Sales force*: one might decrease the commission somewhat and place the amount in a pool that is distributed based on customer comments about specific sales personnel. *Finance office*: bonuses for using company financing should be no more that bonuses based on customer satisfaction ratings. *Detailing*: there must be a measure of quality and detailers should be docked for any problem that results from their lack of attention to detail. *Mechanics*: re-works should dock a mechanics pay and mechanics whose work results in no complaints should receive a significant bonus. *Receptionist/phone service people*: those who answer the phone should be able to gain either performance increases in pay, or bonuses based on customer satisfaction ratings. In general, the approach should be like "teaching to the test." If you want test scores to improve, you teach what will be on the test. If you want measures of customer satisfaction to improve, you reward (or punish) people for those measures.

Case Incident: "Distributing the Raise Pool" (page 469)

1. **What will be the motivational effects on each of the three groups under each method of distribution?** In method one, an equal distribution, the top performers will become less motivated. They will accurately perceive that their extra effort and performance had no influence on their compensation. The bottom performers may feel they can continue to perform poorly, since there is no incentive to do otherwise. Average performers in Method one may be disappointed that they are making no more a raise than poor performers. There should be no improvement in performance. In method 2, the bottom third will be disappointed and possibly angry (even though they may be aware that they are poor performers—they will not appreciate the negative recognition associated with this raise). The middle performers will likely appreciate that they earned more than the lower performers. They may wonder why there is such a large distinction between their raise and the raise of a top performer (why not a 3% difference). It is likely that top performers will feel satisfied they have been rewarded for their work.

In both cases groups will express great concern over the arbitrary nature of dividing the group into equal thirds.

2. **How would you distribute the pool? Why?** There will be some debate in the class response. Most will agree that poor performers are unworthy of a raise. They are not likely to

agree that one third of the company deserves such a rating. They are also likely to suggest a wider range of compensation (a continuous distribution of funds between 0-12%, not just 3-6-9%). The bulk of their arguments will rest on the unfairness of assigning a percentage to poor performance.

Case Application: Bringing the Team Concept into Compensation – Or Not
(page 470)

Sandy Caldwell, the new Human Resources Manager for Hathaway manufacturing, wanted to improve teamwork at every level of the organization. As part of the process of implementing cultural change, Sandy introduced a new pay for performance system. The reaction to the change was immediate and "100 % negative".

1. **Does the pay for performance plan have value?** Management wants to provide incentive for team performance. Their motives are fine. Properly crafted (and with employee involvement) a pay for performance system may add value at Hathaway.

2. **What advice would you give Regina and Sandy as they consider their decision?** Most scholars suggest that pay for performance works best (in the US), when it has both an individual and a team component. Further, Regina and Sandy need to consider ways of engaging the workforce in the design/decision process. This involvement will likely provide better ideas, identify potential problem areas with proposed systems before they are implemented and aid in the implementation process.

3. **What mistakes did they make in adopting and communicating the new salary plan? How might Sandy have approached this major compensation change a little differently?** Sandy failed to involve significant stakeholders in the process. Their input would likely have identified potential weaknesses in her system. Further, by not involving others, the change in pay came largely as a surprise. Employees take their pay seriously; surprises are not welcome. Sandy already had agreement on issues like mission. She could have used that agreement to begin a dialog on linking compensation more directly to the effectively accomplishing the mission.

4. **Assuming the new pay plan were eventually accepted, how would you address the fact that in the new performance evaluation system, employee's inputs affect their peers' pay levels?** Typically, plans have two levels – a team component and an individual component. It is important for the team to realize that the company does best when the whole team succeeds, and that team success also requires individual performance.

Chapter 13
Benefits and Services

In Brief: This chapter discusses the different benefits and services that companies might offer to employees. These are offered to entice employees, retain employees, and to help make them more productive during their service.

Interesting Issues: More and more companies are moving to flexible benefits packages. Students might well be prodded to understand the dynamics driving this, as well as the costs and benefits to the employer.

Lecture Outline

I.   The Benefits Picture Today
Figure 13-1 on Page 476 gives a breakdown of employee compensation.

II.   Pay For Time Not Worked

    A.   Unemployment Insurance
    Table 13-1 on pages 478-479 gives procedures control unemployment costs.

    B.   Vacations and Holidays

    C.   Sick Leave

        1.   Parental Leave and the Family Medical Leave Act of 1993

    D.   Severance Pay

    E.   Supplemental Unemployment Benefits

III. Insurance Benefits

    A.   Workers' Compensation

        1.   Controlling Worker's Compensation Costs

    B.   The High-Performance Organization: Workers' Compensation
    Page 486 of text. See discussion boxes solutions at end of this chapter.

    C.   Life Insurance

    D.   Hospitalization, Medical, and Disability Insurance
    Figure 13-4 on page 488 compares options of traditional, HMO, and PPO.

        1.   Health Maintenance Organizations (HMO)

2. Preferred Provider Organizations (PPO)

3. Reducing Health Benefit Costs

4. Managing Health Care Costs: AIDS

5. Mental Health Benefits

6. The Pregnancy Discrimination Act (PDA)

7. COBRA Requirements

8. Long-Term Care

IV. Retirement Benefits

A. Social Security

1. Retirement Benefits

2. Survivor's or Death Benefits

3. Disability Payments

4. Medicare

B. Pension Plans

1. Defined Benefits

2. Defined Contributions

3. Deferred Profit-Sharing

4. Vesting

5. The Question of Portability

C. Pensions and the Law

1. Employee Retirement Income Security Act (ERISA)

2. Pension Benefits Guarantee Corporation (PBGC)

D. Benefits Trends

1. Golden Offerings

2.   Early Retirement Windows

V.   Employee Service Benefits

A.   Personal Services Benefits

1.   Credit Unions

2.   Counseling Services

3.   Employee Assistance Programs (EAPs)

4.   Other Personal Services

B.   Job-Related Services Benefits

1.   Subsidized Child Care

2.   Elder Care

3.   Subsidized Employee Transportation

4.   Food Services

5.   Educational Subsidies

6.   Family-Friendly Benefits

7.   Research Insight

C.   Executive Perquisites

VI.   Flexible Benefits Programs

A.   Employee Preference for Various Benefits

B.   The Cafeteria Approach
Figure 13-5 on page 501 has advantages and disadvantages of flexible benefits

C.   Information Technology and HR: Computers and Benefits Administration
Page 502 of the text. See discussion boxes solutions at end of this chapter.

D.   Research Insight

E.   How Do Your Benefits Stack Up?

F.   Small Business Applications: Benefits and Employee Leasing
Page 503 of the text. See discussion boxes solutions at end of this chapter.

Figure 13-7 on pages 504-505 shows benefits offerings of six major companies.

Discussion Boxes:

The High-Performance Organization: Workers' Compensation
(page 486)

This box describes the program at Weirton Steel Corporation to control workers' compensation costs. The efforts range from reporting, to management review, to treatment and rehabilitation for those who are injured.

Information Technology and HR: Computers and Benefits Administration
(page 532)

No matter what aspect of benefits you look at, computer applications are playing an important role in the administration. Examples of technology include: telephone-based interactive voice response systems, PC-based systems that allow employees to manipulate benefits choices, and internet systems to provide information.

Small Business Applications: Benefits and Employee Leasing
(pages 503-506)

Leasing employees is an attractive way to reduce costs while actually being able to provide workers with more benefits. This box explains how and why that can be true. However there are a number of issues that need to be considered before taking that step. These are also listed for discussion in this box.

Key Terms

benefits	Indirect financial payments given to employees. They may include health and life insurance, vacation, pension, education plans, and discounts on company products, for instance. (page 476)
supplemental pay benefits	Benefits for time not worked such as unemployment insurance, vacation and holiday pay and sick pay. (page 477)
unemployment insurance	Provides weekly benefits if a person is unable to work through some fault other than his or her own. (page 477)
sick leave	Provides pay to an employee when he or she is out of work because of illness. (page 481)

Chapter 13: Benefits and Services

severance pay

A one-time payment some employers provide when terminating an employee. (page 483)

supplemental unemployment benefits

Provide for a guaranteed annual income in certain industries where employers must shut down to change machinery or due to reduced work. These benefits are paid by the company and supplement unemployment benefits. (page 483)

worker's compensation

Provides income and medical benefits to work-related accident victims or their dependents regardless of fault. (page 485)

group life insurance

Provides lower rates for the employer or employee and includes all employees, including new employees, regardless of health or physical condition. (page 487)

health maintenance organization (HMO)

A prepaid health care system that generally provides routine round-the-clock medical services as well as preventative medicine in a clinic-type arrangement for employees, who pay a nominal fee in addition to the fixed annual fee the employer pays. (page 488)

preferred provider organization (PPO)

Groups of health care providers that contract with employers insurance companies, or third-party payers to provide medical care services at a reduced fee. (page 488)

Pregnancy Discrimination Act

Amendment to title VII of the Civil Rights Act that prohibits sex discrimination based on "pregnancy, childbirth, or related medical conditions." It requires employers to provide benefits - including sick leave and disability benefits and health and medical insurance - the same as for any employee not able to work because of disability. (page 490)

Social Security

Provides three types of benefits: retirement income at age 62 and thereafter; survivor's or death benefits payable to the employee's dependents regardless of age at time of death; and disability benefits payable to disabled employees and their dependents. These benefits are payable only if the employee is insured under the Social Security Act. (page 491)

pension plans

Plans that provide a fixed sum when employees reach a predetermined retirement age or when they can no longer work due to disability. (page 491)

defined benefit pension plan

A plan that contains a formula for determining retirement benefits. (page 491)

defined contribution plan

A plan in which the employer's contribution to employee's retirement or savings funds is specified. (page 492)

deferred profit-sharing

A plan in which a certain amount of profits is credited to each

plan	employee's account, payable at retirement, termination, or death. (page 492)
vesting	Provision that money placed in a pension fund cannot be forfeited for any reason. (page 492)
Employee Retirement Income Security Act (ERISA)	Signed into law by President Ford in 1974 to require that pension rights be vested, and protected by a government agency. (page 493)
Pension Benefits Guarantee Corporation (PBGC)	Established under ERISA to ensure that pensions meet vesting obligations; also insures pensions should a plan terminate without sufficient funds to meet its vested obligations. (page 493)
golden offerings	Offers to current employees aimed at encouraging them to retire early, perhaps even with the same pensions they would expect if they retired at, say, age 65. (page 494)
early retirement window	A type of golden offering by which employees are encouraged to retire early, the incentive being liberal pension benefits plus perhaps a cash payment. (page 494)
employee assistance program (EAP)	A formal employer program for providing employees with counseling and/or treatment programs for problems such as alcoholism, gambling, or stress. (page 495)
flexible benefits program	Individualized plans allowed by employers to accommodate employee preferences for benefits. (page 500)

Discussion Questions:

1. **You are applying for a job as a manager and are at the point of negotiating salary and benefits. What questions would you ask your prospective employer concerning benefits? Describe the benefits package you would try to negotiate for yourself.**
   You should ask about <u>all</u> aspects of the benefits package sufficiently that you will come away knowing exactly what benefits you will and will not have. These can be phrased in many ways, but should cover all areas important to the potential employee. Hopefully students will be far-sighted enough to understand the importance of benefits that might not appear to be critical at this stage of their lives. For example, if students are young and single, they should realize the importance of a good family medical plan as well as a well-funded retirement plan.

2. **Explain how you would go about minimizing your organization's unemployment insurance tax.** Make sure that all your managers understand the unemployment insurance code, train managers and supervisors on discipline and discharge, conduct exit interviews,

verify employment claims, file the protest against a former employee's claim on a timely basis, know your local unemployment insurance official, and audit the annual benefit charges statement. (pages 477-480)

3. **Explain how ERISA protects employees' pension rights.** Under ERISA, pension rights must be vested under one of three formulas. Also, ERISA established the Pension Benefits Guarantee Corporation to help ensure that pensions meet vesting obligations; the PBGC also insures pension should a plan terminate without sufficient funds to meet its vested obligations, (page 493).

4. **In this chapter we presented findings concerning the preferences by age, marital status, and sex for various benefits. What are these findings and how would you make use of them if you were a human resource manager?** The findings are listed at the bottom of page 500 and onto the top of page 501. Human resource managers should use this kind of information to give them a general guideline as to the types of benefits that their work force might prefer. This would be done by analyzing their work force to determine the age, marital status, and sex make-up and then looking to see what the majority of them might prefer. A better approach would be to actually survey the employees to find out their preferences, rather than relying on a sample that might not really represent their employees. Of course, the best option is to offer a cafeteria plan. (pages 500-501)

5. **What is "portability"? Why do you think it is (or isn't) important to a recent college graduate?** Portability is the ability of an employee to take his or her retirement income when they leave an organization and roll it over into a new employer's savings plan or IRA. Today's college graduate may not think about it, but it is important to consider the question of portability. Most college graduates can expect to change employers several times during their career. Having portable retirement plans can help ensure that they end up with a reasonable retirement income. If the plans are not portable, it will take exceptional planning on the employee's part to ensure adequate retirement income. (page 493)

Individual and Group Activities:

1. **Working individually or in groups, compile a list of the perks available to the following individuals: the head of your local airport, the president of your college or university, the president of a large company in your area. Do they have certain perks in common? What do you think accounts for any differences?** There may or may not be any perks in common. The differences are likely to be due to the very nature of the industry in which the organization is engaged, the likely preferences or desires of people who take those positions, and the ability of the organization to provide and fund those types of benefits. (page 500)

2. **Working individually or in groups, contact insurance companies that offer workers' compensation insurance and compile a list of their suggestions for reducing workers' compensation costs. What seem to be their main recommendations?** These recommendations may vary by area and by company, but they are likely to have many parallels to the suggestions provided in the text. Especially consider the suggestions in the

example of Weirton Steel as outlined in *The High Performance Organization* section on page 486. (pages 485-486)

3. **You are the HR consultant to a small business with about 40 employees. At the present time the firm offers only 5 days vacation, 5 paid holidays, and legally mandated benefits such as unemployment insurance payments. Develop a list of other benefits you believe they should offer, along with your reasons for suggesting them.** The specific ones to recommend would depend partly on the profile of the employees of the firm. In the absence of that information, the least costly addition of benefits would be to add some sick leave (or personal days) and consider additional vacation and/or holidays. The next benefit that they might look to would be to add the availability of some kind of health plan that could include a contributory cost to the employee. This would be less expensive to the company and add real value to the employees because of group discounts.

Cases and Exercises:

Experiential Exercise: Benefits Packages (page 508)

This exercise asks students to find out about the benefits packages in small businesses that they have worked in, or in which a friend or family member works. They are then given a scenario and asked to develop, in groups, a benefits plan appropriate for this small business.

Case Incident: "Benefits? Who Needs Benefits?" (page 508)

1. **It would be an exaggeration, of course to imply that the company offers no benefits at all. What sort of benefits must a company like this absolutely provide in order to successfully recruit and retain high-quality employees? Why?** Employees require health benefits. Individual health insurance is very costly, and the risks associated with a catastrophic health event are very high. Most employees want some way to prepare for their future. If a company does not offer a pension plan, employees may expect to receive annual compensation that is sufficiently high as to allow them to develop their own individual program.

2. **What are the advantages and disadvantages of to Fastenol of offering a pension plan? Do you think they should implement one? Why or why not?** The advantage to Fastenol is that employees have come to expect that a company will help them prepare for the future. Advantages of a pension plan are: 1) ability to retain employees, 2) ability to retain employees and 3) possible reduction in salary levels. The disadvantages are 1) additional administrative costs, 2) additional employee expense and 3) on-going costs (hard to disengage from a plan). Fastenol may choose instead to offer a less costly program like a 501 K or an E.S.O.P.

3. **Some critics argue that the labor market is too tight for Fastenol to continue to grow as fast as it has in the past. Critics therefore suggest the company has a dilemma: minimizing benefit's is a good idea because it keeps cost down; however it may soon be less of a good idea if it makes it more difficult to hire good employees. What do**

you think the company should do? Why? The success of a company is dependent in the quality and performance of its employees. Fastenol needs well motivated employees. In a tight labor market, it is common for good employees to receive offers from other companies. Fastenol may discover that in minimizing benefits it will se increased employee turnover.

Case Application: Family Values or Abuse of Benefits? (page 509)

Sarah Conrad was provided a six-week paid pregnancy leave from her firm. She also accepted the company's offer for an additional unpaid six-week leave with continued health and medical benefits. She was offered the opportunity to return to work in a full time or part time position. The company was sufficiently small as to not be required by law to provide these benefits. The provided them because they wanted to be a family oriented business. Sarah repeatedly told her firm she would be returning after her leave, then at the end of her leave, announced her resignation.

1. **Did Sarah Conrad abuse the benefits policy of her employer?** The class may not reach agreement. Those who feel that Conrad abused the policy will note that the company not only lost the time when she was on leave, but it may take them several months to recruit a replacement. Had Sarah announced her intention to leave earlier, then they would have had opportunity to begin searching for a new employee. Some students may go so far as to suggest that the firm was damaged by Conrad's action. Other students may note that Conrad did not step outside the bounds of the policy. Some may feel that she may have feared that had she announced she was leaving the firm may have cancelled her benefits. Others may feel that Conrad simply changed her mind; the experience of being a stay at home mom for 12 weeks reinforced the decision to quit work. (During the discussion, you may try to get the class to separate Conrad's actions, which many students will find inappropriate, from the general issue of providing this benefit to an employee).

2. **If you were Jim, Mike and Dale, would you change your benefits policy?** Some may suggest that the company drop the benefits program altogether, noting they are not legally required to provide it. They may argue that the policy exposes the company to risk (especially the risk that their premiums will increase). Others may suggest that a clause be inserted saying if the employee does not return to work they will be billed for all health premiums.

Chapter 14
Labor Relations and Collective Bargaining

In Brief: This chapter gives a history of the labor movement, outlines the basics of labor law, and reviews the procedures of labor elections, collective bargaining, and contract administration. A look into the future of unionism is also attempted.

Interesting Issues: Union membership has declined in the past few decades. However, unions are targeting professional and other jobs not traditionally unionized. Students need to consider the implications of this shift as well as the dynamics driving it and the likelihood that it will succeed.

Lecture Outline

I.   **Introduction: The Labor Movement**

      A.   A Brief History of the American Union Movement

            1.   1790 Skilled Craftsmen into Trade Unions

            2.   1869 Knights of Labor

            3.   1886 Samuel Gompers AFL

            4.   1930's

                  a.   Roosevelt
                  b.   New Deal
                  c.   National Industrial Recovery Act

      B.   Why Do Workers Organize?
            Table 14.1 on page 518

      C.   What Do Unions Want?

            1.   Union Security

                  a.   closed shop
                  b.   union shop
                  c.   agency shop
                  d.   open shop
                  e.   maintenance of membership arrangement

            2.   Improved Wages, Hours, and Benefits for Members

      D.   The AFL-CIO

            1.   What It Is

2. The Structure of the AFL-CIO

    a. local union
    b. national union
    c. national federation

II. Unions and the Law

A. Background

B. Period of Strong Encouragement: The Norris-LaGuardia Act (1932) and the National Labor Relations or Wagner Act (1935)

    1. Unfair Employer Labor Practices

    2. From 1935 to 1947

C. Period of Modified Encouragement Coupled with Regulation: The Taft-Hartley Act (1947)

    1. Unfair Union Labor Practices

    2. Rights of Employees

    3. Rights of Employers

    4. National Emergency Strikes

D. Period of Detailed Regulation of Internal Union Affairs: The Landrum-Griffin Act (1959)

    1. Bill of Rights for Union Members

    2. Rules for Union Elections

E. Labor Law Today

F. Global HRM: Unions Go Global
Page 527 of the text: See Discussion Boxes solutions at the end of this chapter.

III. The Union Drive and Election

A. Step 1. Initial Contact

    1. Labor Relations Consultants

B. Step 2. Obtaining Authorization Cards

1.   What Management Can Do

C.   Step 3. Hold a Hearing

     1.   Is There Enough Evidence to Hold an Election?

     2.   What is the Appropriate Bargaining Unit?

     3.   Other Issues

D.   Step 4. The Campaign

E.   Step 5. The Election

F.   How to Loose an NLRB Election

     1.   Asleep at the Switch

     2.   Appointing a Committee

     3.   Concentrating on Money and Benefits

     4.   Industry and Blind Spots

     5.   Delegating Too Much to Divisions or Branches

G.   The Supervisor's Role

H.   Rules Regarding Literature and Solicitation

I.   Guidelines for Employers Wishing to Stay Union-Free

     1.   Practice Preventive Employee Relations

     2.   Recognize the Importance of Location

     3.   Seek Early Detection

     4.   Do Not Volunteer

     5.   Beware of the Authorization Cards

     6.   Present Your Case

     7.   Postpone the Election

     8.   Pick Your Time Carefully

            a.   corporate campaign

            b.   boycott

            c.   lockout

    G.   The Contract Agreement Itself

    H.   Changes to Expect After Being Unionized

V.   Contract Administration: Grievances

    A.   The Important Role of Contract Administration

    B.   What Are the Sources of Grievances?

          1.   Always Ask: What Is the Real Problem?

    C.   The Grievance Procedure

    D.   Diversity Counts: Gender Differences in Disputes and Dispute Resolution
           Pages 546-547 of text. See Discussion Boxes solutions at end of this chapter.

    D.   Guidelines for Handling Grievances

          1.   Developing the Proper Environment

          2.   Some Guidelines: Do's and Don'ts

VI.   The Future of Unionism

    A.   Unions Fall On Hard Times

    B.   What's Next for Unions?

        Figure 14-9 on page 549 shows the AFL-CIOs strategy for gaining membership

    C.   Unions and Employee Participation Programs

    D.   The High-Performance Organization: Union-Management Relations
           Page 550 of the text: See Discussion Boxes solutions at the end of this chapter.

    E.   Are Employee Particiaption Programs Unfair Labor Practices?

          1.   Toward "Safe" Participation Programs

Discussion Boxes:

Global HRM: Unions Go Global
(page 527)

This box outlines the efforts that unions are making on the global front. This includes cooperative efforts with unions in other countries to win higher wages there and help keep companies from relocating simply for lower wages. Several examples are cited.

Diversity Counts: Gender Differences in Disputes and Dispute Resolution
(page 577)

This dialogue box discusses some of the differences in types of disputes at work that affect women or men. The study indicates that women are more affected by interpersonal disputes that are not as easily resolved by formal or informal methods ... thus they often take lateral transfers and fall behind in raises or training.

The High-Performance Organization: Uniion Management Relations
(page 550)

The experience of the Department of Energy, Oak Ridge Operations is given as an example of the impact of successful employee-participation-based labor-management relations. This organization has used their TQ efforts as a means to bring labor and management together to work collaboratively.

Key Terms

closed shop	A form of union security in which the company can hire only union members. This was outlawed in 1947 but still exists in some industries (such as printing). (page 520)
union shop	A form of union security in which the company can fire nonunion people, but they must join the union after a prescribed period of time and pay dues. (If they do not, they can be fired.) (page 520)
agency shop	A form of union security in which employees who do not belong to the union must still pay union dues on the assumption that union efforts benefit all workers. (page 520)
open shop	Perhaps the least attractive type of union security from the union's point of view, the workers decide whether or not to join the union; and those who join must pay dues. (page 520)

Norris-LaGuardia Act	This law marked the beginning of the era of strong encouragement of unions and guaranteed to each employee the right to bargain collectively "free from interference, restraint, or coercion." (page 521)
National Labor Relations Board (NLRB)	The agency created by the Wagner Act to investigate unfair labor practice charges and to provide for secret-ballot elections and majority rule in determining whether or not a firm's employees what a union. (page 521)
National Labor Relations (or Wagner) Act	This law banned certain types of unfair labor practices and provided for secret-ballot elections and majority rule for determining whether or not a firm's employees want to unionize. (page 521)
Taft-Hartley Act	Also known as the Labor Management Relations Act, this law prohibited union unfair labor practices and enumerated the rights of employees as union members. It also enumerated the rights of employers. (page 522)
national emergency strikes	Strikes that might "imperil the national health and safety." (page 524)
Landrum-Griffin Act	The law aimed at protecting union members from possible wrongdoing on the part of their unions. (page 524)
union salting	Refers to a union organizing tactic by which workers who are in fact employed full-tim by a union as undercover organizers are hired by unwitting employers. (page 528)
authorization cards	In order to petition for a union election, the union must show that at least 30% of employees may be interested in being unionized. Employees indicate this interest by signing authorization cards. (page 529)
bargaining unit	The group of employees the union will be authorized to represent. (page 530)
collective bargaining	The process through which representatives of management and the union meet to negotiate a labor agreement. (page 538)
good faith bargaining	A term that means both parties are communicating and negotiating and that proposals are being matched with counterproposals with both parties making every reasonable effort to arrive at agreements. It does not mean that either party is compelled to agree to a proposal. (page 538)

voluntary bargaining items
Items in collective bargaining over which bargaining is neither illegal nor mandatory--neither party can be compelled against its wishes to negotiate over those items. (page 540)

illegal bargaining items
Items in collective bargaining that are forbidden by law; for example, the clause agreeing to hire "union members exclusively" would be illegal in a right-to-work state. (page 540)

mandatory bargaining
Items in collective bargaining that a party must bargain over if they are introduced by the other party--for example, pay. (page 540)

mediation
Intervention in which a neutral third party tries to assist the principals in reaching agreement. (page 542)

arbitration
The most definitive type of third-party intervention, in which the arbitrator usually has the power to determine and dictate the settlement terms. (page 542)

economic strike
A stike that results from a failure to agree on the terms of a contract that involve wages, benefits, and other conditions of employment. (page 542)

unfair labor practice strike
A stike aimed at protesting illegal conduct by the employer. (page 542)

wildcat strike
An unauthorized strike occurring during the term of a contract. (page 542)

sympathy strike
A strike that takes place when one union strikes in support of another. (page 542)

corporate campaign
An organized effort by the union that exerts pressure on the corporation by pressuring the company's other unions, shareholders, directors, customers, creditors, and government agencies, often directly. (page 543)

boycott
the combined refusal by employees and other interested parties to buy or use the employer's products. (page 543)

lockout
A refusal by the employer to provide opportunities to work. (page 543)

grievance
Any factor involving wages, hours, or conditions of employment that is used as a complaint against the employer. (page 545)

Discussion Questions:

1. **Explain the structure and purpose of the AFL-CIO.** The AFL-CIO is a voluntary federation of about 100 national and international labor unions in the United States. There are three layers in the structure of the AFL-CIO: the local union, the national union, and the federation. The AFL-CIO acts a spokesman for labor and has accumulated a great deal of political clout. (pages 520-521)

2. **Discuss five sure ways to loose an NLRB election.** The five sure ways to loose an election are listed and described in the text: 1) Asleep at the switch; 2) Appointing a committee; 3) Concentrating on money and benefits; 4) Industry blind spots; and 5) Delegating too much to divisions or branches. (pages 534-535)

3. **Describe important tactics you would expect the union to use during the union drive and election.** Contacting and soliciting employees off the job and during breaks, picketing, using consultants to improve their public image, advertising, news spots, and forming an organizing committee of employees who they feel will be good leaders. (pages 527-533)

4. **Briefly explain why labor law has gone through a cycle of repression and encouragement.** Labor law has gone through cycles of repression and encouragement because of the changing views in congress, the public, and the judiciary on the extent to which legalized collective bargaining is deemed to be a good approach to the economic situation facing the country as well as the views of personal and corporate rights. Changing public attitudes, values, and economic conditions clearly impact labor law, just as they impact law in every area. (pages 521-527)

5. **Explain in detail each step in a union drive and election.** Each step is described in detail in the text: 1) Initial contact involves the union determination of the employees' interest in organizing and forming an organizing committee; 2) Obtaining authorization cards is where the union seeks to obtain enough signatures on authorization cards to petition the NLRB to conduct an election; 3) Holding a hearing is done by the NLRB to determine the appropriate bargaining unit and the legality of the authorization cards; 4) The campaign is where both sides present the issues to convince employees to vote one way or the other; and 5) The election is conducted by the NLRB and is by secret ballot. (pages 527-533)

6. **What is meant by good faith bargaining? When is bargaining not in good faith?** Good faith bargaining means that both parties are communicating and negotiating and that proposals are being matched with counterproposals with both parties making every reasonable effort to arrive at agreements. Ten examples of violations of good faith bargaining are listed on pages 538-539.

7. **Define impasse, mediation, and strike, and explain the techniques that are used to overcome an impasse.** Impasse occurs when the parties are not able to move further toward settlement. Mediation is intervention in which a neutral third party tries to assist the principals in reaching agreement. A strike is the withdrawal of labor. An impasse might be overcome through mediation, fact-finders, arbitration, or the economic pressures of a strike or lock-out. (pages 541-542)

Individual and Group Activities:

1. **You are a supervisor in a small manufacturing plant. The union contract covering most of your employees is about to expire. Working individually or in groups, discuss how to prepare for union contract negotiations.** You need to know what is good faith bargaining and what constitutes a violation of good faith bargaining. Although as a supervisor you will not likely be involved in the negotiations, you can commit violations of good faith bargaining like making a unilateral change in working conditions, or the commission of an unfair labor practice. Also you need to be a vehicle to give information about employee attitudes and concerns to those conducting the bargaining. The list on page 541 gives a good summary of who to prepare for bargaining. (pages 540-541)

2. **You are the president of a small firm of 30 employees. While you are not unionized, you would like to have an appeals process that would serve a purpose similar to that of a grievance procedure. Working individually or in groups, prepare a presentation describing what this appeals process might entail.** Because the perview of grievances is "any factor involving wages, hours, or conditions of employment that is used as a complaint against the employer" you must be very careful to **not** involve employees in the formation and running of the grievance procedure to avoid the appearance of a sham union (pages 551-552). The procedure should have several stages in which the employee can appeal to higher and higher levels of management to hear their case. In some cases, a well constructed grievance procedure can involve the rotating selection of a panel of peers to hear and decide the case. (pages 546-547)

Cases and Exercises:

Experiential Exercise: Union Orgainizing (page 554)

This exercise sets up a situation in which a supervisor has reported to the HR director that there have been unionization efforts in her department. She describes what has happened, what employees have said, and what other supervisors have said and done. The question for the students is what HR Director Art Tipton should do next.

The most pressing issue to deal with right away is the apparent fact that supervisors are engaging in unfair labor practices. Art must hold a meeting with supervisors immediately to instruct them in what they can and cannot do. Lists of items are on the bottom of page 529, and on pages 535-536. After everyone has been instructed on what they can and cannot do, the organization can turn to the issue of how to avoid becoming unionized. There are two lists in the text that help with this: "How to Loose an NLRB Election" on pages 534 & 536 as well as "Guidelines for Employers Wishing to Stay Union-Free" on pages 536-537.

Case Incident: Disciplinary Action (page 555)

1. **As the arbitrator, do you think the employer had just cause to discipline the employee?** No, the employer did not have just cause. The task of directing and ordering employees to do tasks is a management task and is not a union task. Management abrogated its responsibilities in asking the union to do a task that is a reserved management right and duty.

2. **If the union's opposition to the Quest for Quality program encouraged the employees not to participate, why shouldn't the union be held responsible for directing the employees to attend?** As stated in the previous question, directing employees is a management duty and right, it is not one that can be abrogated to the union at will. Management should direct the employees to attend, then discipline them if they do not. The union is not required to be supportive of all management programs or directions.

Case Application: Empowerment through Assignment Flexibility (page 556)

The Paper Corporation of America (PCA) had just negotiated an agreement with two unions. Under the agreement, workers from one union could perform tasks normally done by members of the other union. The purpose was to improve the flexibility of the workforce to increase productivity. Workers shared the financial reward of improvements in productivity. Workers were allowed to turn down work they considered unsafe. The first week, two workers turned down an assignment of unloading a truck as they said it was unsafe. The two had in fact unloaded the truck in the past under the old contract. Management accused them of just being lazy. The flexibility committee was asked to render an opinion on the incident by answering the following questions:

1. **Were the actions of the set-up supervisor correct? Why or why not**. The set-up supervisor was certainly correct in asking them to load the truck. There is no evidence from the case that the supervisor that the supervisor knew the workers had unloaded that truck before. The criteria for AF required the supervisor to get agreement on five questions. The workers disagreed with question one.

2. **Were the actions of he two shipping department workers correct? Why or why not?** The two workers, if they had safely unloaded trucks in the past were not acting in good faith. (There is no evidence in the case as to whether unloading the truck requires any special skills). This leads to the impression that the workers were in fact just declining to do an assignment because they didn't want to do it.

3. **Were the actions of the department head correct? Why or why not?** The department head acted in a very confrontational manner. The AF process is clearly defined as requiring five steps. The department manager seems to be putting pressure on employees to say yes, even if they have reservations. He is in effect adding a sixth step, "Every time you say no your performance will be reviewed."

4. **What would have been a correct way for each of the above parties to act?** The supervisor may have asked for clarification from the employees as to what specifically they

felt was unsafe about the job. If the supervisor knew they had done the work before, he should have asked a few questions to probe why they could do that work then and not now. If he felt he was being mislead by the employees he could have mentioned that he planned on discussing this matter further with his management team. The shipping workers either needed to identify what specifically they felt was unsafe or to accept the work. If the work was unsafe, they could have been trained in the knowledge, skills and abilities to safely unload the truck so they could do it in the future. The department chair needed to separate his reaction to the two employees from the policy issue of how to treat all employees. By pressuring workers to say yes or be reviewed, he may be pressuring workers to take tasks with which hey feel a little uncomfortable. This could lead to resentment and lower performance, or worse, industrial accidents.

5. **Do you think this incident will affect the successful use of AF in the mill? Why or why not?** Yes, workers may feel they are being coerced or forced into being flexible. The literature strongly suggests that coercion increases resistance to change. The action of the department head might dramatically slow the change process.

6. **What effects do you think the successful use of AF, allowing workers to participate in decision making, will have on empowerment and organizational culture of PCA in the long term?** If implemented successfully, the company should see an improvement in productivity. This improvement may show up in a variety of ways. For example, the cross training the occurs may make it unnecessary for the company to hire replacement help to cover vacations. It may reduce overtime by allowing slack resources to be redirected toward overworked areas. The workers may begin to get a better sense of how the company operates and how individual jobs contribute to overall goals. This could in turn improve job satisfaction and retention.

7. **What does the case tell use about implementing change, particularly empowerment, in organizations?** Change is not easy. It requires the cooperation of the parties involved. It does not happen merely by issuing a policy statement. Once a change plan has been devised it will likely still face resistance in some sectors. Management should anticipate the types of resistance to change and discuss how they will be handled before the change is implemented.

Chapter 15
Employee Safety and Health

In Brief: This chapter outlines occupational safety law and then discusses causes of accidents and how to prevent them. There is also a section devoted to employee health.

Interesting Issues: The role of OSHA is somewhat controversial in today's society. Some feel it is an intrusion by a bungling governmental bureaucracy that doesn't really understand the nature of work and jobs, while others view it as the *only* check and balance available to help save employees' lives and limbs.

Lecture Outline

I.   **Why Employee Safety and Health Are Important**

II. **Basic Facts About Occupational Safety Law**

   A.   Purpose

   B.   OSHA Standards
        Figure 15-1 on page 564 gives an example of an OSHA standard.

   C.   OSHA Record keeping Procedures
        Figure 15-2 on page 565 shows what accidents must be reported under OSHA.

   D.   Inspections and Citations

        1.   Inspection Priorities

        2.   The Inspection Itself

        3.   Citations and Penalties

   E.   Responsibilities and Rights of Employers and Employees

        1.   Dealing with Employee Resistance

   F.   The Changing Nature of OSHA

   G.   Small Business Applications: OSHA and the Small Business
        Page 570 of the text. See discussion boxes solutions at the end of this chapter.

III. **The Supervisor's Role in Safety**

   A.   Top-Management Commitment

IV. **What Causes Accidents?**

Chapter 15: Employee Safety and Health

    A.   The Three Basic Causes of Accidents

    B.   Unsafe Conditions and Other Work-Related Accident-Causing Factors

        1.   Three Other Work-Related Accident Factors

    C.   What Causes Unsafe Acts (A Second Basic Cause of Accidents)

        1.   Personal Characteristics and Accidents

        2.   What Traits Characterize "Accident-Prone" People?

            a.   vision
            b.   age
            c.   perceptual versus motor skills
            d.   vocational interests
            e.   summary

        3.   Research Insight

V.   How to Prevent Accidents

    A.   Reducing Unsafe Conditions

    B.   Reducing Unsafe Acts Through Selection and Placement

        1.   Screening for the Traits Listed Above.

        2.   The ADA and Safety

    C.   Reducing Unsafe Acts Through Posters and Other Propaganda

    D.   Reducing Unsafe Acts Through Training

    E.   Reducing Unsafe Acts Through Incentive Programs and Positive Reinforcement

        1.   The New Safety Program

        2.   Reinforcement and Safety

    F.   Reducing Unsafe Acts Through Top-Management Commitment

    G.   Reducing Unsafe Acts by Emphasizing Safety

    H.   Reducing Unsafe Acts by Establishing a Safety Policy

    I.   Reducing Unsafe Acts by Setting Specific Loss Control Goals

J. Reducing Unsafe Acts by Conducting Safety and Health Inspections

K. Reducing Unsafe Acts by Monitoring Work Overload and Stress

L. Safety Beyond the Plant Gate

M. Global HRM: Safety at Saudi Petrol Chemical
Page 581 of the text. See discussion boxes solutions at the end of this chapter.

N. Controlling Worker's Compensation Costs

1. Before the Accident

2. After the Accident

3. Facilitate the Employee's Return to Work

O. The High-Performance Organization: Safety Programs
Page 582 of the text. See discussion boxes solutions at the end of this chapter.

VI. Employee Health: Problems and Remedies

A. Alcoholism and Substance Abuse

1. Various Techniques Used to Deal with These Problems

2. Workplace Substance Abuse and the Law

B. The Problems of Job Stress and Burnout

1. Reducing Job Stress

C. Burnout

1. Research Insight

D. Asbestos Exposure at Work

E. Video Display Health Problems and How to Avoid Them

F. AIDS and the Workplace

G. Workplace Smoking

1. The Nature of the Problem

2. What You Can and Cannot Do

3. Smoking Policies

H. Dealing With Violence at Work

  1. The Nature of the Problem

  2. Reducing Incidents of Workplace Violence

  3. Heightened Security Measures

  4. Improved Employee Screening

  5. Workplace Violence Training

  6. Enhanced Attention to Retaining Employees

  7. Dealing with Angry Employees

  8. Legal Constraints on Reducing Workplace Violence

I. Diversity Counts: In Occupational Safety and Health
    Page 596 of the text. See discussion boxes solutions at the end of this chapter.

Discussion Boxes:

Small Business Applications: OSHA and the Small Business
(page 570)

This box discusses the differences in OSHA inspections between a large firm and a small firm. The main point of the discussion is that small firms who are fined need to not cave in right away, but negotiate for reductions in the penalties. Some good statistics are given to support this case.

Global HRM: Safety at Saudi Petrol Chemical
(page 581)

This box describes the safety program at this company in Saudi Arabia. Besides actively involving all employees in the safety program, they also require employees to report every incident and near miss of a safety nature. This allows the company to track trends and develop recommendations.

The High-Performance Organization: Safety Programs
(page 582)

Human Resource Management

Prior to the 1990s, Dayton Parts, Inc. had no worker safety programs. New management and high injury costs prompted the company to actively pursue and manage employee safety. This box describes in some detail the initiatives they have developed.

Diversity Counts: In Occupational Safety and Health
(page 596)

This box discusses the large number of women who are killed by assault while on the job. While 18% of males who die on the job are murdered, for women who die on the job, 39% of them are victims of assault.

Key Terms

Occupational Safety and Health Act	The law passed by congress in 1970 "to assure so far as possible every working man and woman in the nation safe and healthful working conditions and to preserve our human resources." (page 563)
Occupational Safety and Health Administration (OSHA)	The agency created within the Department of Labor to set safety and health standards for almost all workers in the United States. (page 563)
citations	Summons informing employers and employees of the regulations and standards that have been violated in the workplace. (page 567)
unsafe conditions	The mechanical and physical conditions that cause accidents. (page 571)
unsafe acts	Behavior tendencies and undesirable attitudes that cause accidents. (page 573)
burnout	The total depletion of physical and mental resources caused by excessive striving to reach an unrealistic work-related goal. (page 588)

Discussion Questions:

1. **How would you go about providing a safer environment for your employees to work in?** Providing a safer work environment for employees starts with the three E's – education, engineering, and enforcement. Top management commitment to providing a safe work environment, and the resources to achieve it, is critical. Reducing accidents usually boils

down to two thrusts: reducing unsafe conditions and reducing unsafe acts. This question is focused towards unsafe conditions. (page 575)

2. **Discuss how to minimize the occurrence of unsafe act on the part of your employees.** The text lists 10 different ways to help reduce unsafe acts. Answers should reflect at lease a majority of these. (pages 575-580)

3. **Discuss the basic facts about OSHA – its purpose, standards, inspection, and rights and responsibilities.** The purpose of OSHA is "to assure so far as possible every working man and woman in the nation safe and healthful working conditions and to preserve our human resources." The basic purpose of OSHA is to set safety and health standards and to ensure compliance through inspections and reporting. The standards are contained in five volumes covering general industry standards, maritime standards, construction standards, other regulations and procedures, and a field operations manual. The standards are very complete and seem to cover just about any hazard one could think of. Standards are enforced through a series of inspections and, if necessary, citations. OSHA may not conduct warrantless inspections without an employer's consent. It may inspect after acquiring a search warrant. An authorized employee representative also must be given the opportunity to accompany the officer during the inspection. Employees are protected under the act from discrimination for exercising their disclosure rights. Employers are responsible for being familiar with OSHA standards and for brining conditions into compliance. (pages 563-570)

4. **Explain the supervisor's role in safety.** Beyond trying to make the workplace safe, the basic aim of the supervisor is to instill in workers the desire to work safely. Then, when needed, enforce safety rules. (page 570)

5. **Explain what causes unsafe acts.** People are the main cause of unsafe acts. Some researchers say that certain personal characteristics are the basis for behavior tendencies that result in unsafe acts. There are several human traits that contribute to accident proneness and they are listed on page 574. There is a list on page 573 of some examples of unsafe acts. (pages 573-575)

6. **Describe at least five techniques for reducing accidents.** The text lists 10 techniques: 1) selection and placement; 2) posters and other propaganda; 3) training; 4) incentive programs and positive reinforcement; 5) top-management commitment; 6) emphasizing safery; 7) establishing a safety policy; 8) setting specific loss control goals; 9) conducting safety and health inspections; 10) monitoring work overload and stress. These are detailed on pages 575-580

7. **Analyze the legal and safety issues concerning AIDS.** The legal issues employers must deal with concern their responsibilities in dealing with AIDS sufferers. Case law is only now developing, but several tentative conclusions are warranted: 1) you cannot single out any employee for AIDS testing; 2) You can require a physical exam that includes AIDS testing as a condition of employment, but you may not be able to refuse to hire someone whose test is positive; 3) Mandatory leave of someone with AIDS cannot be required unless their work performance has deteriorated. (pages 590-592)

8. **Explain how you would reduce stress at work.** Both environmental and personal factors can lead to job stress. If individuals are feeling dysfunctional levels of stress, the work schedule, pace of work, job security, and number or nature of clients, modifications in these factors should be made. Because personal factors influence stress, health and exercise programs can be promoted. Sometimes counseling should be offered, especially through an EAP, or a job more suitable to the individual should be found. Supervisors should monitor performance to identify symptoms of stress, and inform the employee of organizational remedies that may be available, such as job transfers or counseling. (pages 587-589)

Individual and Group Activities:

1. **Working individually or in groups, answer the question, "Is there such a thing as an accident-prone person?"** Yes and No. While most psychologists agree that accident proneness is not universal, most do agree that accident proneness is situational. For example, *personality traits* may distinguish accident prone workers on jobs involving risk, and lack of *motor skills* may distinguish accident prone workers on jobs involving coordination. Many human traits have been found to be related to accident repetition in specific situations. (page 574)

2. **Working individually or in groups, use the checklist in this chapter to identify safety hazards in your college or university.** There is a checklist (Figure15-4) on page 572, but students are better directed to Appendix 15-1 beginning on page 603. Check student answers for thoroughness and reasonability. Sometimes students will be unreasonably strict in their interpretations of standards.

Cases and Exercises:

Experiential Exercise: Interpreting Safety Standards (page 600)

This exercise is the same as the item just above (#2 in the Individual and Group Activities). Again, it is best to use the checklist on pages 603-606.

Case Incident: The New Safety Program (page 600)

1. **How should a laundry go about identifying hazardous conditions that should be rectified?** There are a number of common methods to accomplish this. One is to use an outside consultant who specializes in this area. Another method is to take the OSHA and EPA guidelines for this industry and perform and internal audit of operations.

2. **Would it be advisable for a firm to set up a procedure for screening out accident-prone individuals?** There are a number of issues here. One likely question from students is whether accident-prone behavior can change with training or incentives. In most cases, training and incentives can resolve the problem. Some students may argue that screening-out employees who are accident-prone raises ethical issues.

3. **How would you suggest that owners get all employees to behave more safely at work? Also, how would you advise them to get those who should be wearing goggles to do so?** Most firms in this case would use a combination of training and incentives to induce safe behavior. It is also common to include safe behavior as part of an individual's performance appraisal. Similar approaches would be applied to the goggles problem. (Students are likely to suggest that workers be shown an interview with a worker who was severally injured though the failure to use safety glasses. Others will argue that the task can be accomplished less graphically).

Case Application: Introducing Ergonomics: What Went Wrong? (page 601)

After reading an article about savings generated at the US Post Office through better work design, HR Manager Roger Scanlon puts forth a plan for a more ergonomically designed work setting at Harbor.

1. **Did anything go wrong? Is so, what?** The method Roger used heightened employee awareness of problems in their working conditions. It also made it culturally acceptable to discuss those problems in the open. The problem may not have changed, but awareness and discussion of the problem did.

2. **What elements of Roger's plan could be improved?** Roger may wish to implement his plan incrementally, focusing first on employees or departments that have had difficulties in this area or had reduced outcomes due to absenteeism, etc.

3. **What do you think accounts for the increase in reported illness and injury?** Employees may not have related their aches and pains to workplace related issues. As a result of their training, they now felt comfortable blaming their employer.

4. **Given your answer to Question 3, do you think Harbor should go ahead with the renovation?** There are several issues here: actual working conditions and problems, and employee perceptions. On the primary issue of working conditions, the case seems to indicate the conditions need improvement. At this stage, canceling those improvements might increase employee dissatisfaction. Harbor needs to consider what its communication and implementation strategy will be so as to not convey to employees that they have been negligent about working conditions until now.

Chapter 16
Managing Human Resources in an
International Business

In Brief: This chapter outlines some of the HR problems and issues involved with international businesses. Subject coverage includes inter-country differences, using selection to improve international assignments, and training and maintaining international employees.

Interesting Issues: Many companies are desiring to rotate managers through international assignments, but find that work visa requirements of the host countries (including the U.S.) can sometimes greatly hinder these efforts.

Lecture Outline

I.   **Introduction: The Internationalization of Business**

    A.   The Growth of International Business

    B.   HR and the International Business Challenge

    C.   New Destinations
        Figure 16.1 on pages 618-619 shows destinations for foreign assignments

    D.   How Intercountry Differences Affect HRM

        1.   Cultural Factors

        2.   Economic Factors

        3.   Labor Cost Factors

        4.   Industrial Relations Factors

        5.   The European Community (EC)

II. **Improving International Assignments Through Selection**

    A.   Why International Assignments Fail

    B.   International Staffing: Sources of Managers

    C.   International Staffing Policy

    D.   Selecting International Managers

        1.   Adaptability Screening

2.	International Selection in Practice

3.	Diversity Counts: Sending Women Managers Abroad
Page 626 of text. See discussion boxes solutions at the end of this chapter.

## III.	Training and Maintaining International Employees

A.	Orienting and Training Employees for International Assignments

B.	International Compensation

1.	The Balance Sheet Approach

2.	Incentives

3.	Beyond Compensation

C.	Performance Appraisal of International Managers

D.	International Labor Relations

E.	Safety and Fair Treatment Abroad

F.	Repatriation: Problems and Solutions

Discussion Boxes:

Diversity Counts: Sending Women Managers Abroad
(pages 626-627)

This box points out that women are often overlooked or discounted for international assignments. This discussion points out that most of the assumptions which result in decisions to exclude are invalid assumptions.

Discussion Questions

1. **You are the president of a small business. What are some of the ways you expect being involved internationally will affect your business?** Being involved internationally can affect virtually every aspect of your business. It can affect the growth of your business due to additional markets, it can affect costs of doing business, and it can affect every aspect of HRM as outlined on pages 616-620.

2. **What are some of the specific uniquely international activities an international HR manager typically engages in?** 1) Formulating and implementing HR policies and activities in the home-office of a multinational company. This HRM manager would engage in selecting, training, an transferring parent-company personnel abroad and formulating HR

policies for the firm as a whole and for its foreign operations. 2) Conducting HR activities in the foreign subsidiary of an MNC is another form. Again, local HR practices are often based on the parent firm's HR policies, fine tuned for local country practices. (page 615)

3. **What intercountry differences affect HRM? Give several examples of how each may specifically affect HRM.** 1) Cultural Factors. U.S. managers may be most concerned with getting the job done. Chinese managers may be most concerned with maintaining a harmonious environment. And Hispanic managers may be more concerned with establishing trusting, friendship relationships. 2) Economic Factors. U.S. economic systems tend to favor policies that value productivity while more socialistic countries like Sweden would favor policies that prevent unemployment. 3) Labor Cost Factors. Mexican labor costs (low) can allow inefficiencies of labor, while German labor costs (high) might require a focus on efficiency. 4) Industrial Relations Factors. German law requires that workers have a vote in setting policies while in Japan the employees do not have a say, but the government may have a say in establishing policies. 5) The European Community. The EC will gradually reduce the differences between member countries. (pages 616-620)

4. **You are the HR manager of a firm that is about to send its first employees overseas to staff a new subsidiary. Your boss, the president, asks you why such assignments fail, and what you plan to do to avoid such failures. How do you respond?** Estimates say that 20% to 25% of all overseas assignments fail. Reasons include: inability of spouse to adjust, managers' inability to adjust, other family problems, managers' inability to cope with responsibility. We will need to select a manager that displays: adaptability and flexibility, cultural toughness, self-orientation, others-orientation, perceptual ability, and has a family with adaptability. (pages 620 & 621)

5. **What special training do overseas candidates need? In what ways is such training similar to and different from traditional diversity training?** It is suggested that a four-step training approach be taken: 1) training focused on the impact of cultural differences and their impact on business outcomes. 2) focused on attitudes and aims at getting participants to understand how attitudes (both positive and negative) are formed and how the influence behavior. 3) factual knowledge about the target country. and 4) skill building in areas like language and adjustment and adaptation skills. This training is different from traditional diversity training in the last two steps, which are not normally part of diversity training. In addition, traditional training and development is needed as with any other manager. (page 626)

6. **How does appraising an expatriate's performance differ from appraising that of a home-office manager? How would you avoid some of the unique problems of appraising the expatriate's performance?** A major difficulty is: Who actually appraises the performance? (cultural differences could affect it) There are five suggestions: 1) Stipulate the assignment's difficulty level; 2) Weight the evaluation towards the on-site manager's appraisal; 3) Have a former expatriate advise the home-site manager in his or her evaluation; 4) Modify the normal performance criteria to fit the position and characteristics of the locale; 5) Attempt to give credit for insights, not just measurable criteria. (pages 629)

7. **What do you think accounts for the fact that worker participation has a long and relatively extensive history in Europe? How do you think this relatively extensive participation affects the labor relations process?** The history of Europe is unique and different from other areas of the world. The development of concern for employee rights and

participation in the determination of the organization's directions are deeply rooted. This extensive participation affects the labor relations process deeply. The process is not an adversarial bargaining process as we are used to in the U.S., but often is dictated by law and or involves the worker's representatives in the decision-making process. (page 631)

8. **As an HR manager, what program would you establish to reduce repatriation problems of returning expatriates?** The programs listed on page 632 give a good summarization of the types of programs and activities that should be established to assure a smooth repatriation. (page 632)

Individual and Group Activities

1. **Give three specific examples of multinational corporations in your area. Check the library or Internet or with each firm to determine in what countries these firms have operations and explain the nature of some of their operations, and whatever you can find out about their international HR policies.** The examples will vary according to what companies have operations in your area. This can be an exciting opportunity for students to find out more about companies and what they are doing beyond your immediate geographic area.

2. **Choose three traits useful for selecting international assignees, and create a straightforward test (not pencil and paper) to screen candidates for these traits.** There are an infinite number of responses that you might get to this question. First, make sure that the traits either are on the list on page 624, 625, or are reasonable and logical traits that would be useful. Second, assure that the tests that the students develop are ones that will actually identify the presence of these traits.

3. **Describe the most common approach to formulating expatriate pay. Use a library source to determine the relative cost of living in five countries as of this year, and explain the implications of such differences for drafting a pay plan for managers being sent to each country.** The most common approach is to equalize purchasing power across countries, a technique known as the balance sheet approach. The basic idea is that each expatriate should enjoy the same standard of living he or she would have had at home. (page 628)

Cases and Exercises:

Experiential Exercise: Compensation Incentives for Expatriate Employees (page 635)

This exercise forces students to think realistically about the compensation problems with expatriate employees. The rankings will vary, but students should be prepared to defend their rankings with reason and logic. Similarly, while the described "effects on compensation" may vary, they should be reasonable and logical. When discussing the problems that the higher level of compensation might create, do not forget: 1) jealousy of other employees, 2) problems of adjustment when repatriation occurs, and 3) whether even this level will be adequate to entice employees to take the foreign assignments.

Compensation incentives for expatriate employees

(completed table)

Your Rank	Issues	Description	Effect on Compensation	% +or-
(example)	Health care	Physicians and hospital do not meet western standards.	Make contingency money available to fly expatriate to closest country with Western style health care)	+5
3	Family life	There are no English language schools for children—children of expatriates will need to attend private boarding schools.	Employees will need higher salaries to pay school tuition.	+10
2	Inflation	Target country currency is unstable. Currency may inflate by as much as 20% per month.	Payment might need to be paid in $US rather than local currency (functions as a bonus…as inflation increases, $$ become more valuable).	=
4	Infrastructure	The expatriate will not be able to have his or her own phone or TV.	Creates a perceived hardship; may require additional compensation to attract an appropriate employee.	+10
1	Political risk	Assigned country faces the risk of political upheaval.	Clearly a hardship condition; employee will expect higher pay. Arrangements should be made for off-shore banking, access to cash and unusual repatriation expenses.	+50

Directions
Divide the class into small teams. Ask each team to perform the following tasks:

1. **Rank order the issues from one to five (number one being the most important).**
There will be some variation here, though political risk should rank the highest.

2. **Consider that each employee has a base salary equal to their US compensation. You may add from 0% to 50% for each item on the list.**

Note that in the above example, inflation can be handled without increasing the salary.

Answer the following discussion questions as a larger group:

1. **How much did you need to increase compensation overall to satisfy the expected needs of your expatriate workers?** In the above example, 75%.

2. **What problems might this level of compensation create?** Might make your firm less competitive. Might create difficulties with national employees in the host country who are making just the base salary. Might create difficulties when you try to repatriate an employee back to U.S. wages.

Chapter 16: Managing Human Resources in an International Business

Case Incident: "Boss, I Think We Have a Problem" (page 636)

1. **Based on the chapter and case incident, compile a list of 10 international HR mistakes Mr. Fisher has made so far.** Among his mistakes: Fisher has not properly identified candidates; cultural sensitivity, interpersonal skills and flexibility have not been included as required job skills; there is no system in place to assess candidates for proper skills; the company does not have realistic cost projects for cross-border operations; the company has not determined whether it would be cost effect to have an expatriate manager; there are no assignment letters documenting the scope of the job; there is no international compensation system in place; the company has not taken into account differences in foreign expenses; the company has not taken into account foreign taxes; there is no formal relocation assistance program in place; the company has not considered the importance of family support; there is no cultural orientation program in place for expatriate mangers or their family members; among others.

2. **How would you have gone about hiring a European sales manager? Why?** I would have investigated the market to determine the appropriate level of compensation and benefits. Expropriate compensation packages should consider tax equalization clauses or other measures for dealing with differing costs of living. The company should also have retained consul on European labor laws/ practices. The location of the office should be carefully selected for favorable labor and tax laws. Like Fisher, I would have wanted a large pool of potential applicants, but given Fisher's inexperience, he may have benefited from the use of an outside agency (search firm). Finally, Fisher's stereotypes of European managers may have clouded his judgement with his existing pool of applicants.

3. **What would you do now if you were Mr. Fisher?** Fisher needs to seek legal consul in regard to his labor situation. He is likely in the wrong. In which case, he will need to reinstate the employees and apologize. He will in all likelihood need to start over and find an appropriate sales manager with knowledge of the local culture and business practices.

Case Application: Taking a Fast Boat to Nowhere (page 636)

Two years after sending and ambitious and highly regarded executive to Hong Kong to oversee a major expansion into Asia, the US firm, Bandag, Inc., closed its Chinese office. In the process the laid off their former "star" employee Gerald Borenstein.

1. **What uncontrollable factors contributed to the crisis in Borensteins's career?** The economic downturn in Asia put enormous pressure on prices and virtually eliminated any opportunity for profit. Further, since all competitors where in the same position, it intensified competition. Also, the man who hired Borenstein and to some extent championed this expansion retired, leaving Borenstein with without an advocate in the home office.

2. **Over what factors did he have control?** He selected new more expensive offices before the company had successfully expanded. Further, he paid salaries for four engineers when only one was needed in anticipation of an economic upturn. Borenstein also chose to stop attending home office meetings saying the 18 hours of travel weren't worth a few hours of home office meetings.

3. **Whether you think they would changed the eventual outcome or not, how might Borenstein have handled the controllable factors differently?** It is likely that only a few executives in the home office had the level of international field experience possesses by Borenstein. Without an advocate in the home office, Borenstein needed to spend time educating his home office colleagues on the specifics of the Asian opportunity. Further, he should have sought greater advice and consent before hiring significant staff based on his forecast. By making that decision in isolation from the home office, he became an easy target for blame once the project failed.

4. **What, if anything, could Bandag have done differently to minimize the impact of the economic downturn on Borenstein and his family?** Bandag should have realized the cross border operations involve higher levels of risk. They could have guaranteed Borenstein a position in the home office, or outplacement in the event they closed the venture. (There were also business and financial strategies they could have chosen that would have minimized the effect of the Asian currency crisis). Bandag should have been able to anticipate that the currency crisis in Southeast Asia would carry over to Hong Kong and made arrangements to scale back their operations for a year. This would have allowed Bandag to establish a long term presence in Asia, one of the largest and fastest growing markets in the world.

Video Guide to accompany
Human Resource Management, 8/e
Gary Dessler

Skills Live!
Part-Ending Segments (Tape 1 of 2)

QuickTakes Video is a small, fictional television production company that produces short films, videos and news segments for corporate clients. In these short segments, you will meet owner Hal Boylston, and watch as he interacts with his employees on various issues. Following each vignette is a question and answer session with management expert and author, Gary Dessler. **NOTE TO INSTRUCTOR: Stop the *Skills Live!* video following each skit's questions for students to answer. Afterwards, continue the video. Prof. Dessler will give the suggested answers on the video.** The segments follow:

A Case of Sexual Harassment – 9:30
End of Part I (Chps 1-2): Introduction
This video gives an example of sexual harassment at work. Student should watch the 5-minute video case and then answer the questions in groups before watching Dessler's 4:30-minute response.

Interviewing Job Candidates – 9:45
End of Part II (Chps 3-6): Recruitment and Placement
A job interview is simulated in this segment. The poorly handled interview between Hal Boylston and a prospective employee seems haphazard and both parties appear unprepared for what is happening. Students will watch the nearly six-minute skit, answer questions on effective interviewing, and then listen to Dessler's response.

Appraising Performance – 11:00
End of Part III (Chps 7-10): Training and Development
This segment demonstrates the need for some method of recordkeeping in matters of performance appraisal. The manager shown discusses an employee's review with her boss and then with the employee. The review detours drastically from a discussion on performance to a heated, emotional debate on the employee's worth. Students will answer questions on how the conflict might have been avoided.

Establishing Pay Plans – 10:30
End of Part IV (Chps 11-13): Compensation
Changing family and living conditions have forced an employee to petition Hal Boylston for a pay raise. Neither QuickTakes' owners nor the employee have any data about internal or external equity. It is emphasized to students that most large companies have established pay scales and many employees are not able to negotiate their pay in this manner.

Labor Relations – 8:00
End of Part V (Chps 14-15): Labor Relations and Employee Security
An encounter between the supervisor and a union employee over the supervisor's dissastifaction with the employee's work habits is portrayed. What results is the

enforcement of a disciplinary action that may or or may not be allowable under the union contract.

Managing HR in International Business – 10:45
End of Part VI (Chp 16): International Human Resource Management
While QuickTakes is a small U.S.-based company, it does maintain a one-man office in London to oversee its shoots throughout Europe and Africa. Issues of equity in compensation, paid/unpaid vacation and time off, and autonomy between employees in the London and New Jersey offices are raised.

Small Business 2000 Video for HRM
Company Cases (Tape 2 of 2)

Chapter 1 – Rocky Mountain Helicopters – 12:00
Rocky Mountain Helicopters is a small business that has seen major changes, including rapid growth, a financial crisis, going public, and a change in top management. Yet, RMH faces all the HRM issues of a large company. The company must recruit and train employees, compensate them, and manage promotion and terminations systems.

Chapter 3 – Cowgirl Cream – 11:31
Change is hot at Cowgirl Enterprises, where new products aren't the only segment influenced by the innovation-friendly atmosphere. With non-traditional job characteristics and job titles, like "Trail Boss" (Operations Manager), Cowgirl has cut costs by outsourcing and reallocating resources.

Chapter 4 – Community Insurance – 9:48
Using mentoring and his community ties, an African-American entrepreneur shows how his tactics attracted applicants. But demonstrating that there are career opportunities for minorities in the insurance industry wasn't enough. He has devised ways to retain employees, decrease turnover, and provide training for students and future employees.

Chapter 5 – Anne McGilvray, Inc. – 8:20
Job previewing and tough interviewing are at the heart of McGilvray's hiring process. Anne checks references, credit histories and even psychological profiles, before taking candidates out on some calls. In order to become successful sales reps, they must be somewhat of an entrepreneur, she says, running their accounts like small businesses.

Chapter 7 – The French Laundry – 9:47
Past failures have taught owner Thomas Keller how not to run his next restaurant. After hiring consultants, Keller focused on training his employees. The restaurant now boasts having North America's best chef and best pastry chef on staff, who teach their 20 assistant chefs how to create the ultimate dining experience.

Chapter 8 – Calise Bakery – 8:34
Tiny Calise Bakery was in financial trouble. Declaring bankruptcy would have been cheaper than renewing the company, but the management team made it work. Renewing in phases – paying close attention to cash management, upgrading technology and improving training, Calise now clears $13 million and has 170 employees.

Chapter 10 – Dell's Lemonade – 9:15

A former dentist with over 50 years of small business management experience, reflects on his career and his franchising operation. He's been successful starting businesses, but he's learned to give control to those with greater expertise in fields he might not have. The result is his consulting to his group of franchises.

Chapter 12 – Cactus and Tropicals – 12:24

This Utah-based nursery and floral-design company wanted to attract the best candidates for each position. But keeping them meant establishing an attractive incentive plan. By sharing the company's profits, employees are encouraged to consistently innovate, increase sales and improve the overall productivity.

Chapter 13 – Halliday Real Estate – 10:52

At 87, Halliday has built her company with savings from her earlier days. Her informal work environment has attracted and helped retained many lifelong employees – one is also 83-years-old! But informal management styles don't always work. Halliday gave 49% of her shares in the company to those employees who helped build it with her.

Chapter 15 – Maple Court Apartments – 9:15

Being in a wheelchair has made designer Phil Maleris sensitive to the difficulties of working and living in non-disabled accessible spaces. When he created Maple Court Apartments, the goal was to make the complex totally "barrier free" and welcoming for both its residents and its employees.

SB2000 Video: Rocky Mountain Helicopters
Chapter 1: The Strategic Role of HRM

Be aware of these issues as you watch the video:
- What role does HRM play in a small business?
- In what ways is the strategic role of HRM in a small business similar or identical to its role in a larger business?
- What costs are associated with not having an effective HR system?

1. What were some of the major transitions at Rocky Mountain Helicopters where HR issues would have likely surfaced?
2. Rocky Mountain Helicopters would be considered a small business. What types of HR issues does a small business like RMH face?
3. How critical are human resources to RMH's success?

Answers to Chapter 1 Video Questions
Rocky Mountain Helicopters

1. What were some of the major transitions at Rocky Mountain Helicopters where HR issues would likely have surfaced?

Rocky Mountain Helicopters has gone through a number of major stages including rapid growth, a financial crisis, going public, a change in top management, Chapter 11 reorganization, change in business direction and diversification into pre-hospital medical services. A number of HR issues would surface at each of those changes. For example, during a period of high growth, HRM would be involved heavily in recruiting. During a period of decline the HR staff might aid in downsizing decisions. Chapter 11 requires a company to reorganize for greater efficiency. HRM would likely be consulted on job redesign and organizational structure issues. Finally, the diversification of the business would involve HR in the forecasting of future HR needs, identifying and recruiting potential employees, etc.

2. Rocky Mountain Helicopters would be considered a small business. What types of HR issues does a small business like RMH face?

Rocky Mountain Helicopters faces all the issues a larger firm would face. The company must forecast HR needs, recruit, orient and train employees, compensate them and motivate them to good performance, handle employee benefits, manage appraisal and promotion systems and terminations. While there may be structural differences in HRM in small companies (fewer HR professionals, outsourcing of some functions), the tasks of HR in small businesses is identical to that of large businesses.

3. How critical are human resources to Rocky Mountain Helicopters' success?

Three characteristics of Rocky Mountain Helicopters' business suggest that human resources are critical to their success. First, they provide 24 hour a day service in a life-and-death environment. Employee error cannot be allowed. Employees must be motivated to work at peak levels on every assignment. Second, there is a pervasive use of high technology in this business. One characteristic of high technology is rapid change. This implies a high need for on-going training. Finally, the business has very demanding customers. Where there are demanding customers, the only way to keep customers satisfied is to provide services that meet or exceed customer expectations. Any companies that wish to may purchase helicopters and enter into this business. The key to success in this business is not the physical assets, but the effective use of human resources.

Skills Live! Video: A Case of Sexual Harassment
End of Part 1: Introduction

Be aware of these issues as you watch the video:
- What are some elements that create a hostile work environment?
- What are the responsibilities of Hal Boylston, the company owner?
- What evidence will Kim need to do to prove a case of harassment?

1. Is Brad about to create a hostile work environment?
2. What should Hal do now?
3. What should Kim do? If Kim decides to lodge a formal complaint, what would she have to prove?
4. What laws apply to situations like the one at QuickTakes?

SB2000 Video: Cowgirl Cream
Chapter 3: Job Analysis

Be aware of these issues as you watch the video:
- In what ways is a virtual organization different than a traditional organization?
- What is the role of job design in a virtual organization?
- Is the requirement for job design in a virtual organization greater or lesser than in a traditional organization?

1. What does the "cowgirl" metaphor convey? How does the idea of a "cowgirl" affect job design?

2. What is the role of outsourcing in job design? What use did Cowgirl make of outsourcing?

3. What are some of the unique issues that influence job design at Cowgirl?

Answers to Chapter 3 Video Questions
Cowgirl Cream

1. What does the "cowgirl" metaphor convey? How does the idea of a "cowgirl" affect job design?

The idea of a cowgirl is intended to convey a number of attributes that the founder hopes will strike a resonant chord with customers. Those attributes are: independence, resourcefulness, saying in the saddle (persistence), taking the reins (leadership), making good use of natural resources, and driving your own life. Cowgirl influenced the company to develop non-traditional job titles and job characteristics. Nearly all jobs are part time. Jobs include titles like "head rustler" (cash flow management), and "trail boss" (operations manager).

2. What is the role of outsourcing in job design? What use did Cowgirl make of outsourcing?

In designing jobs, a company must first decide what roles it intends to fulfill and what roles could be better handled by outside organizations. The requirements for job design are somewhat different. On one hand, the company needs to be very specific about the outcomes it wishes to achieve in terms of quantity, quality, time and cost. It can be considerably less specific in terms of how employees meet those outcomes. The final job design is largely passed on to the supplier. Cowgirl used outsourcing in its manufacturing operations. Cowgirl made the decision that the company could not afford to have staff equal in skill and knowledge to Rocky Mountain Natural Laboratories. Yet it needed the results of those skills to compete. It paid its supplier to develop the product, manufacture it and bottle it. In a similar move, once Cowgirl designed the packaging job for the cake products, it found it could not find suitable numbers of employees with flexible capacity. They chose to use the Boulder County Jail inmates as their workforce.

3. What are some of the unique issues that influence job design at Cowgirl?

Cowgirl is in part a virtual organization. It has a core set of tasks that it accomplishes internally, largely with part time employees. Cowgirl needs to identify tasks/jobs and determine which of those will be handled internally. Among the considerations for job design mentioned in the video are:
1) full time vs. part time employment
2) use of technology
3) image/design issues
4) high volumes of production with high variability
5) difficulty in finding skilled labor
6) a need to handle rapid business growth.

SB200 Video: Community Insurance
Chapter 4: Personnel Planning and Recruiting

Be aware of these issues as you watch the video:
- There are major differences in the way individuals go about the process of finding a career for themselves.
- To what extent can an organization influence someone's career choice?
- Many organizations need to actively recruit prospective employees. What attributes make an organization attractive to a job candidate?

1. What made insurance an attractive career for Milt Moses? What role did Moses' formal training play in his career choice?
2. What methods did Moses' company employ to attract job applicants?
3. What role does the formal mentoring program play in Moses' recruitment program?

Answers to Chapter 4 Video Questions
Community Insurance

1. **What made insurance an attractive career choice for Milt Moses? What role did Moses formal training play in his career choice?**

Moses wanted a career where he could support his family. Moses had seen his own insurance agent's career prosper. Moses had trained for a career in broadcasting but had seen few African Americans in the field. In insurance, he felt that his race would not be a limiting factor in his career. While Moses did not enter the career for which he initially trained, his training was likely still valuable. As part of his studies Moses undoubtedly studied communications skills that he would use for the balance of his career.

2. **What methods did Moses' company employ to attract job applicants?**

Moses was an aggressive recruiter. The video notes the use of the following techniques: recruited from schools; advertised in newspapers; asked clients for referrals; contacted friends; sought referrals from relatives of existing employees and neighbors of existing employees; and spoke with church groups. Moses also worked at retention efforts—making his insurance business a good place to work—so that he would have lower turnover and thus lower recruiting needs.

3. **What role does the formal mentoring program play in Moses recruiting program?**

The mentoring program appeared to fulfill three roles. Moses saw a need to develop human resources for the industry as well as for his company. He wanted to send a clear message that there were still great career opportunities for minorities in the insurance industry. So at one level, there was a symbolic value of the mentoring program—symbolizing the attainability of success. Second, he wanted to provide training so those candidates from his mentoring program had a better chance for success in the field of insurance. Third, the mentoring program established a link between his firm and the students in the program. Moses and his company were clearly presenting themselves as leaders in the field.

SB2000 Video: Anne McGilvray, Inc.
Chapter 5: Employee Testing and Selection

Be aware of these issues as you watch the video:
- In what ways was McGilvray in a position to evaluate the likelihood of success of a new representative?
- Why would McGilvray use an outside consultant to help in testing (why not just go with her hunch)?

---

1. What are the essential ingredients for success in a manufacturer's rep organization?

---

2. What role do realistic job previews play in Anne's recruiting process?

---

4. What strengths do you see in Anne's recruiting process? What might you change?

Answers to Chapter 5 Video Questions
Anne McGilvray, Inc.

1. What are the essential ingredients for success in a manufacturer's rep organization? In what ways was Anne qualified to assess their abilities?

Manufacturer's reps are primarily sales professionals. Anne needed to recruit, train and retain sales professionals who could recruit, train and retain professionals in their territories. Anne was in a position to evaluate them based on her own success as a rep. More importantly, she had been hiring reps for a period of years. At the time of this video, she had 90 reps working on behalf of 200+ manufacturers. Her customer base was estimated at over 65,000 customers (mostly small retailers).

2. What role did realistic job previews play in Anne's recruiting process?

Anne seemed to go out of her way to explain to prospective reps the nature of the work. She gave courses for prospective reps and took them on sales calls. She looked for a two-year minimum commitment and informed prospective reps that the entire first year was usually quite difficult. She also informed prospective reps about the difficult cash flows in the first year and the likelihood that they would need significant financial resources before starting their business. Her goals seemed to be:
   1) to recruit people who enjoyed the business and what not be put off by the work itself.
   2) recruit people who had the resources to stay with it for two years.
   3) to reduce the expense the comes from reps who fail.

3. What strengths do you see in Anne's recruiting process? What might you change?

In addition to her realistic job preview (which is a clear strength), Anne also employs testing. Even though Anne has had a successful career in this field, she still uses testing to screen candidates. She used a consulting psychologist to develop a profile of her most successful reps. Potential candidates are then compared to that profile. In particular, Anne pays attention to service orientation. On the down side, Anne still admits failures. In several cases she had candidates say they had the financial resources to be a rep, only to drop out after a short period due to poor cash flow. Anne could easily ask for a commercial credit report and bank references to externally validate the financial capacity of her prospective reps.

Skills Live! Video: Interviewing Job Candidates
End of Part II: Recruitment and Placement

Be aware of these issues as you watch the video:
- Has Hal established a good rapport? What could he do to establish rapport?
- Is Hal well prepared for the interview?
- How does the candidate handle the interview?

1. What do you think of the interview so far?
2. What are hypothetical questions like Hal's questions to Mary called?
3. Did Hal follow most of the guidelines for conducting an interview?
4. What guidelines has he ignored?

SB2000 Video: The French Laundry
Chapter 7: Training and Development

Be aware of these issues as you watch the video:
- The role can "star" employees and managers play in the training process.
- The role of performance standards.
- What role if any can failure play in the development process?

---

1. What role do performance standards play at the French Laundry?

2. What role did failure play in the learning experience of Thomas Keller? Why do you think his failures did not discourage him?

3. What role do star employees play in the training process at the French Laundry? In what ways might mentoring be inferior to using training professionals? In what ways is it superior?

Answers to Chapter 7 Video Questions
The French Laundry

1. What role do performance standards play at the French Laundry?

The French Laundry has a very clear expectation as to what makes a great dining experience. They appear to have standards for food and service. For food, the tape noted the following expectations: great meals, perfect ingredients, great preparation and employees with a passion for excellence. In the service area, the tape noted high levels of personal service and interaction with customers. There was also a notable level of professionalism in the staff. For example, the person who took phone reservations had a professional job title, "reservationist."

2. What role did failure play in the learning experience of Thomas Keller? Why do you think his failures did not discourage him?

Keller had two failures in the restaurant business prior to his success at the French Laundry. While this would discourage many (most) people, Keller had decided to use both as learning experiences. He analyzed his past performance and identified those things he did well as well as the areas where he failed. In looking at his next restaurant, Keller focused more attention on the areas where in the past he had weak performance. He also brought in outside help in some of the areas where he lacked expertise. As a result of his careful self-reflection, Keller's confidence increased after his failure because he was able to identify the causes of his failure and take steps to overcome them.

3. What role do star employees play in the training process at the French Laundry? In what ways might mentoring be inferior to using training professionals? In what ways is it superior to using training professionals?

The French Laundry can boast of having the best chef in North America and the best pastry chef. The 20 cooks know they are working with the world's best. They understand that if they learn everything that these mentors have to offer that they will on track to becoming great in their own right. Training professionals can be superior to experts in the techniques of assessment and training delivery. They are seldom content experts. Training professionals usually work in concert with content experts. Experts can be superior to training professionals in at least one way. By virtue of the recognition they have received in their field prior to conducting training, experts have earned the respect of the trainees. They have no need to prove themselves. Under these circumstances, experts can initially expect the rapt attention of their trainees.

Name _____

SB2000 Video: Calise Bakery
Chapter 8: Management Renewal

Be aware of the following issues as you watch the video:
- What was the initial condition of the bakery?
- What steps did management take to turn the business around?
- What role did human resources play in the renewal of Calise Bakery?

1. What was the condition of Calise Bakery before renewal? Describe the company at that time.
2. What process or sequence did Calise's management team use in renewing their business?
3. What were the outcomes of Calise's renewal efforts?

Answers to Chapter 8 Video Questions
Calise Bakery

1. What was the condition of Calise Bakery before renewal? Describe the company at that time.

The company was virtually bankrupt. In fact the owners felt it would have been easier to declare bankruptcy then to renew the business. At the time, the bakery was a retail operation including door to door sales. In the first two years of the renewal, the management team had to let go of six employees. The tasks these employees performed still needed to be done resulting in very long working hours for the owners.

2. What process or sequence did Calise's management team use in renewing their business?

Calise employed a three stage process. First, the company analyzed and replaced business processes they considered as being antiquated. They paid especially close attention to the management of cash flow (short term financial obligations). Second, they upgraded the bakery with modern technology and automation (One machine could now produce 840 loaves of bread an hour). Finally, they invested extensively in people. This investment including in-house training and outside training experiences. For example, bakers were sent to the prestigious American Institute of Baking to receive expert training.

3. What were the outcomes of Calise's renewal efforts?

Calise Bakery was successfully renewed. At the time of the case, the company had grown to $13 million in annual revenues. The company had over 170 employees. In addition to its financial growth, Calise had been cited for its award winning quality products by several important magazines.

SB2000 Video: Dell's Lemonade
Chapter 10: Managing Careers

Be aware of the following issues as you watch the video:
- Pay attention to the differences that occur in an entrepreneur's career and an employee's career
- Notice the career transition stages
- Consider the knowledge and skills Angelo acquired in his fifty years with Dell's

1. What stages did Angelo go through in his career? To what extent were those stages planned?

2. What knowledge and skills did Angelo acquire early in his career? How valuable were those skills?

3. How did Angelo's experience make him an excellent franchiser? Why would someone pay a royalty to "rent" Angelo's expertise?

Answers to Chapter 10 Video Questions
Dell's Lemonade

1. **What stages did Angelo go through in his career? To what extent were those stages planned?**

Angelo began his career over 50 years ago. He served a short time in the military. Following the war, the government paid to send Angelo to dental school. He formed a dental business with a partner who ended up stealing his money. He left the dental business to go into the bowling alley business with his father. (He took over when his father decided he couldn't get along with the pin boys). Because there was no air conditioning (making the business seasonal), Angelo opened a lemonade stand on the lot next to his business to help summer cash flows. With the revenues from that, Angelo delved into production engineering and created mechanical processes for improving quality. He branched into mobile sales of the product through custom trucks. When he reached the limit of what he could do on his own, he began to sell franchises to attract people with sufficient talent and commitment to help him succeed in his business. Angelo's early career was largely unplanned. He happened upon his career choice by accident. Many of the skills Angelo needed he developed informally—cash flow management, production engineering, and quality management. He had the self awareness to hire qualified people to fill in areas where he would not be able to develop the skills (e.g., Ph.D. in food science).

2. **What knowledge and skills did Angelo acquire early in his career? How valuable were those skills? Could Angelo have developed them more quickly?**

Angelo developed deep skills in two areas of the business: products and processes. Angelo developed standards for product quality and innovated to be able to produce product at a high quality and uniform level with some efficiency. He also developed processes for marketing the product, handling localized production, managing cash flows, and operating the day to day business. Individually, these skills were not necessarily of high value. In fact, one could argue that individually these skills were very common and therefor would be priced low in the market. However, Angelo possessed the full set of skills necessary to be successful in his endeavor. Angelo did not have a formal education, did not have a clear career path, nor did he have a mentor. Any of those career strategies would likely have accelerated his career path. If he had a clear strategy from the beginning, he could have directed his learning toward specific skills. A mentor may have also been able to accelerate his timetable.

3. **How did Angelo's experience make him an excellent franchiser? Why would someone pay a royalty to "rent" Angelo's expertise?**

Angelo possessed the full set of skills needed to run a local lemon-ice type operation. More importantly, Angelo possessed the ability to package those skills and rent them to other entrepreneurs. Angelo was very systematic; he was able to package a complete system for the franchisee. The franchisee would gladly pay Angelo a royalty. The royalty is a payment for the skills and knowledge Angelo acquired in the 50-year period he had been in business. By paying a royalty, his franchisees could avoid the mistakes that most small businesses make. He provided them a quality product and a working system (and according to the tape, he provided it at very favorable terms).

Skills Live! Video: Appraising Performance
End of Part III: Training and Development

Be aware of these issues as you watch the video:
- The thoroughness or lack of thoroughness of the appraisal form and process.
- The preparation for the review.
- How the performance review is handled.

1. What mistake is Karen (the out-of-house sales representative) making in giving Tom such a high rating?
2. What would you have done different with this appraisal?
3. Was Janet fully prepared for this interview?
4. What would you have done if you were in Janet's place?
5. What would you have done if you were in Tom's place?

SB2000 Video: Cactus & Tropicals
Chapter 12: Pay-For-Performance and Financial Incentives

Be aware of the following issues as you watch the video:
- Can incentives work alone, or do they need the support of a strong leader or organizational culture?
- Why might someone choose to work for a smaller business like Cactus & Tropicals when they could work for a large firm?
- To what extent does a firm's pay and incentive systems help attract quality employees.

1. What incentives did Cactus & Tropicals provide? Did the compensation system stand on its own, or did it require other management tools?
2. To what extent was the compensation system directed toward narrow outcomes vs. broad outcomes? Why would this type of system work for Lorraine's company?
3. How does the compensation system aid Cactus & Tropicals' quest for competitive advantage?

Answers to Chapter 12 Video Questions
Cactus & Tropicals

1. **What incentives did Cactus & Tropicals provide? Did the compensation system stand on its own, or did it require other management tools?**

In addition to a creative and relatively autonomous working environment, Cactus and Tropicals had a profit sharing plan. The performance based pay component was based on improvement in net income. Employees were provided access to financial data from prior years and the current year. The employees split a profit pool equal to 40% of the increase in net income over the prior year. (The tape gave an example that the group had budgeted a $16,000 pool, but their performance led to a $40,000 pool). The system required significant training. Essentially, employees were asked to think like general mangers with P&L responsibility. As such, they also needed to know a good amount about the fit between their job and those of the other employees. This allowed employees to work on processes that would improve the whole company's performance, not just their departments.

2. **To what extent was the compensation system directed toward narrow outcomes vs. broad outcomes? Why would this type of system work for Lorraine's company? Are there any noticeable problems in Lorraine's pay plan?**

The pay system was aimed at very broad outcomes (improvement in net profit year to year). There were no sub-targets of market share, sales growth, customer satisfaction or any other intermediate goals. All employee activity was targeted toward this single measure of company performance. In general, this system worked well in Lorraine's company because: she supported the system with proper training and communication; the employees were able to see the link between their performance and rewards, and it supported a culture of self-directed work teams and relative autonomy that was consistent with Cactus & Tropicals desired work culture.   There were some weaknesses in the Cactus & Tropical plan: 1) its reliance on a single measure of performance and 2) the employees shared a higher level of risk in the event of poor performance and 3) a possible bias toward short term results. In the event there was an event outside the employee's control, the employees could end up doing a good job and receiving no bonus. There is nothing in the system to moderate this. Also, the employees can exaggerate a bonus by taking short term actions for a few years that strengthen the bottom line but reduce investment in the business.

3. **How does the compensation system aid Cactus & Tropicals' quest for competitive advantage?**

The system aids competitive advantage in three ways. First, it acts as an incentive to attract high quality people. Second, the system causes individual employees to act like owners (reducing the agency problem). The cross training associated with this results in staff that know each other's business. Finally, the incentive system rewards entrepreneurial behavior at all levels of the organization.

Name _____

SB2000 Video: Ebby Halliday Real Estate
Chapter 13: Benefits and Services

Be aware of the following issues as you watch the video:
- Pay attention to the differences that occur in a small business environment.
- Itemize the benefits you perceive in working for a company like Halliday Real Estate.
- Consider the distinction between formal and informal benefits at Halliday.

1. Why did Ebby Halliday feel she could start her career working on straight commission?

2. What benefits did Halliday provide her employees? Which of these benefits would you describe as more likely to occur in a small business environment or as an "informal" benefit?

3. Which organization is more likely to have informal benefits, a small business or a large business? Based on your review of Halliday's business, what are some disadvantages of informal benefits versus formal benefits?

Answers to Chapter 13 Video Questions
Ebby Halliday Real Estate

1. **Why did Ebby Halliday feel she could start her career working on straight commission? Would most people have been able to start their career the same way?**

Halliday had been a successful commodities investor (cotton futures market). She had built a very large savings base from which to operate. Most people do not start from a base of savings. In fact, many recent college graduates start from a base of debt in the form of student loans.

2. **What benefits did Halliday provide her employees? Which of these benefits would you describe as more likely to occur in a small business environment or as an "informal" benefit?**

Halliday had given up 49% equity in her company to share with employees as she felt they had built the company. This was clearly an informal benefit (it was not contracted that she give up her equity. Halliday appeared to be a very 'healthy" place to work (informal). There was not a mandatory retirement age (formal benefit). Halliday herself was 87 and her controller was 83, eighteen years older then the typical retirement age. Also, employees routinely received training and technological assistance to upgrade their performance (formal).

3. **Which organization is more likely to have informal benefits, a small business or a large business? Based on your review of Halliday's business, what are some disadvantages of informal benefits versus formal benefits?**

A small business is more likely to offer informal benefits. A large business has formalized their benefits program so that it can be administered efficiently and equitably. Many of the most important benefits provided by Halliday were informal, most notably, the equity she provided her employees and the "healthy" work environment. The are several disadvantages to informal benefits: 1) there is no requirement that the company provide them and 2) there is no formal system to assure their equitable distribution. (Note that once Halliday decided to give equity, she would have had to develop a formal system for its distribution. The informal part of the benefit is that she could have chosen to not give it.

Skills Live! Video: Establishing Pay Plans
End of Part IV: Compensation

Be aware of these issues as you watch the video:
- What about internal equity?
- What about external equity?
- What is the total compensation package?

1. Has Kim mentioned her performance or types of equity?   If so, what are they?
2. What should Hal and Karen have done before giving a raise to Kim?
3. How could QuickTakes improve the way it sets pay rates?
4. What role do benefits play in compensation packages?

Name _____

SB2000 Video: Maple Court Apartments
Chapter 15: Employee Safety and Health

Be aware of the following issues as you watch the video:
- Pay attention to the differences in building design that are required to accommodate disabled employees.
- Consider the role that building design plays in attracting and retaining disabled employees.
- Determine if Phil Maleris achieved his goals in building design.

1. What are some of the attributes of a "barrier free" office or housing complex? Why are these attributes important?

2. In what ways did Maleris go beyond the requirements of barrier free access in his design of Maple Court Apartments? How would these features benefit a disabled person?

3. What advantages could a company gain by creating a safe and conducive work environment for disabled employees?

Answers to Chapter 15 Video Questions
Maple Court Apartments

1. **What are some of the attributes of a "barrier free" office or housing complex? Why are these attributes important?**

The case notes several attributes, including: 6-inch wide shoulders, no curbs, automatic doors, wide hallways (enough to allow two wheel chairs to pass without bumping each other), roll-in showers, lowered switches & fuse boxes, lowered thermostats, lower height to shelving and lower cabinets. These attributes allow a disabled person to function with assistance from other people.

2. **In what ways did Maleris go beyond the requirements of barrier free access in his design of Maple Court Apartments? How would these features benefit a disabled person?**

All entries were barrier free; the disabled were not relegated to a single entrance. By using a ranch style design, no one was living above a disabled person. The units for disabled persons were interspersed among more typical units. Maleris purposefully chose to provide a low density housing arrangement (it would not look like a government housing project. He saved 19 of the 24 trees on the site. Maleris had created an environment where the disabled could be totally integrated into the life of the community. There was no visual segregation of the disabled at any level of the project.

3. **What advantages could a company gain by creating a safe and conducive work environment for disabled employees?**

First, they would be in compliance with the law. The ADA (Americans with Disabilities Act) requires companies to make some accommodations for disabilities. Second, there is a large pool of talented prospective employees who have been frozen out of the work force by their disabilities. The government official in the tape noted that 80% of disabled Americans are not working. Of those, 30% are on welfare. Third, people with disabilities want to work. They do not wish people to feel sorry for them or to have people serve them. Finally, as disabled employees are taken off welfare and moved to productive jobs, it reduces the potential tax burden on businesses.

Skills Live! Video: Labor Relations
End of Part V: Labor Relations and Employee Security

Be aware of these issues as you watch the video:
- What limits does the union contract place on Hal?
- Are John's actions probably covered by the contract?

1. What should Hal do when the union calls?
2. What shouldn't he do?
3. What steps should Hal have taken earlier to protect his company?
4. Explain why you think Jim joined a union.

Skills Live! Video: Managing HR in an International Business
End of Part VI: International HRM

Be aware of these issues as you watch the video:
- What are the differences between job expectations in the U.S and abroad?
- How does culture influence attitudes/perspectives towards work?
- Is equal compensation a corporate responsibility in a multinational organization?

1. Should employees in the U.S. and the UK work the same number of hours/days?
2. Should they have the same benefits? Why or why not?
3. How can the differences be reconciled?
4. If Tim stays on staff, how could he be compensated at the same rate as U.S. employees? Would it simplify payroll if all employees were in the U.S.?
5. If Tim freelances, what problems might that pose for QuickTakes?
6. What would you do about paying Tim?